THE ESSENTIAL

Australian Shepherd

CHAPTER ONE:

Getting to Know Your Australian Shepherd 1

CHAPTER TWO:

Homecoming 7

CHAPTER THREE:

To Good Health 15

CHAPTER FOUR:

Positively Nutritious 33

CHAPTER FIVE:

Putting on the Dog 41

CHAPTER SIX:

Measuring Up 47

CHAPTER SEVEN:

A Matter of Fact 56

CHAPTER EIGHT:

On Good Behavior .64

CHAPTER NINE:

Resources 87

Index 91

The Australian Shepherd's Senses

SIGHT

Australian Shepherds can detect movement at a greater distance than we can, but they can't see as well up close. They can also see better in less light, but can't distinguish many colors.

SOUND

Aussies, like all dogs, can hear about four times better than we can, and they can hear high-pitched sounds especially well.

TASTE

Australian Shepherds have fewer taste buds than we do, so they're likelier to try anything—and usually do, which is why it's important for their owners to monitor their food intake. Dogs are omnivorous, which means they eat meat as well as vegetables.

TOUCH

Aussies are social animals and love to be petted, groomed and played with.

SMELL

An Australian Shepherd's nose is his greatest sensory organ. A dog's sense of smell is so great he can follow a trail that's weeks old, detect odors diluted to one-millionth the concentration we'd need to notice them, even sniff out a person underwater!

Meet the Australian Shepherd

■ Australian Shepherds, commonly called "Aussies," are categorized by the American Kennel Club as members of the Herding Group.

■ Aussies were bred to herd livestock. If they see sheep, geese, chickens, goats, ducks—even a group of children—their instinct is to start herding them.

■ Despite his name, the Australian Shepherd did not originate in Australia. Many historians have theorized that the breed came to America with early settlers from Europe. Others believe the breed originated in Spain, went to Australia, then came to California during the Gold Rush of 1849.

■ Australian Shepherds love to play ball, go for hikes, catch flying disks and participate in obedience, agility, tracking, herding and carting events. While suited to many activities, they are not "hyper" dogs, but they do need to have a job, something to keep their minds challenged and their bodies busy.

■ The Australian Shepherd's coat color is black, blue merle, red merle and red with or without white markings and/or tan points.

■ The Aussie's water-resistant coat enables him to adapt to various conditions and to work long hours in harsh weather.

■ The Aussie's coat sheds, but it is very easy to keep up, does not mat and does not need to be trimmed.

■ The Australian Shepherd is an amazingly strong dog for his size, but can easily learn to control his power, using it only when required.

■ Australian Shepherds are instinctively protective and make great guard dogs.

Consulting Editor
IAN DUNBAR PH.D., MRCVS

Featuring Photographs by
MARY BLOOM

Howell Book House
An Imprint of Macmillan General Reference USA
A Pearson Education Macmillan Company
1633 Broadway
New York, NY 10019

The Essential Australian Shepherd is a revised edi-
tion of *The Australian Shepherd: An Owner's Guide
to a Happy Healthy Pet*, first published in 1997.

Library of Congress Cataloging-in-Publication
Data
        The essential Australian shepherd /
consulting editor, Ian Dunbar ; featuring photographs by Mary Bloom.
            p.   cm.
    Includes bibliographical references and index.
    ISBN 1-58245-026-9
    1. Australian shepherd dog.   I. Dunbar, Ian.
    SF429.A79E77 1999
    636.737—dc21   98-45863
                                            CIP

Manufactured in the United States of America
10 9 8 7 6 5 4 3 2 1

Series Director: Michele Matrisciani
Production Team: Carrie Allen, Toi Davis, Clint
    Lahnen, Stephanie Mohler, Dennis Sheehan,
    Terri Sheehan
Book Design: Paul Costello
Vetrinary Exam performed by David L. Ouart,
    D.V.M.
Photography page 77 courtesy of Diana
    Robinson.

ARE YOU READY?!

☐ Have you prepared your home and your family for your new pet?

☐ Have you gotten the proper supplies you'll need to care for your dog?

☐ Have you found a veterinarian that you (and your dog) are comfortable with?

☐ Have you thought about how you want your dog to behave?

☐ Have you arranged your schedule to accommodate your dog's needs for exercise and attention?

No matter what stage you're at with your dog—still thinking about getting one, or he's already part of the family—this Essential guide will provide you with the practical information you need to understand and care for your canine companion. Of course you're ready—you have this book!

CHAPTER ONE

Getting to Know Your Australian Shepherd

The Australian Shepherd is, first and foremost, a herding dog. Although many Aussies are involved in other activities and dog sports, the breed's herding heritage is still strong, even in those Aussies that have never seen a sheep.

A Herding Dog as a Pet

Herding instincts, chase instincts and prey drive are closely related, and can cause a dog to chase anything that moves: sheep, cattle, cats, cars or children. Naturally, this can be a good talent when developed properly in a working herding dog, but it can cause problems when the dog chases cars or children or kills livestock.

Aussies with Children

Aussies are loyal family members and active, energetic companions for

1

young children. As with any dog, you are responsible for making sure dog and child interact peacefully. Your Aussie must be trained to respect even the little people in his life, and your children must learn how to treat their dog properly. Ear pulling, tail grabbing and teasing will try the patience of the most even-tempered dog. Older children who have been taught properly can be excellent with dogs. If you are unsure about the situation, supervise their interactions until you are secure.

PROTECTIVE INSTINCTS

The Australian Shepherd's instinct to guard his property also come from his herding instincts. When there is no flock to protect, the Aussie protects his people instead. This protective instinct can be seen in everyday situations, such as the dog's active barking when someone approaches the house, or his low growl when a stranger approaches the family children. If you want your Aussie to be accepting and friendly to family, it is your job to train him to be accepting and friendly.

A STRONG DRIVE TO WORK

All Australian Shepherds need to have a job. Because the breed was derived from herding dogs and was designed to work, Aussies need an occupation, something to keep the mind challenged and the body busy.

The Australian Shepherd's protective instinct, combined with his herding instincts and desire to work, make the breed valuable to people who need a working dog.

A bored Aussie will become a bad Aussie, guaranteed. Many bored Aussies dig up the backyard, uproot plants, chew on the lawn furniture, bark incessantly and try to escape from the yard.

There are quite a few different jobs that you can give your dog. Obedience training can give him some structure in his life and teach him to work for you and to listen to your commands. Teach him to bring in the morning newspaper and to find your slippers and your keys. Teach him to find family members by name. Teach him to play Frisbee, or find a dog training club in your area that can teach both of you something new, like agility, flyball or scent hurdle races.

LIVING WITH AN AUSTRALIAN SHEPHERD

The Australian Shepherd is a medium sized dog, averaging between 45 and 60 pounds. That means a 45- to 60-pound dog curled up by your side on the sofa or stretched out across your feet. Although an Australian Shepherd is not a large dog, his heart is. Everything an Aussie does, he does in a big way.

CHARACTERISTICS OF AN AUSTRALIAN SHEPHERD

active

protective

intelligent

needs stimulating activity and strenuous exercise

sheds a lot

affectionate

loyal to those they consider friends

A POWERFUL DOG

The Australian Shepherd is an amazingly strong dog for his size, both in physical strength and in stamina. Aussies love to play athletic games,

As a result of their strong desire to work, Australian Shepherds are happiest when they are kept busy.

3

When an Aussie loves you, he loves you totally and unconditionally.

such as Frisbee, in which they can use their strength, stamina and athletic prowess. Because of his strength, an Aussie without training could easily jump up and knock down a child, a senior citizen or even an unprepared adult. With training, Aussies can learn to control their power, using it only when required.

AN INTELLIGENT DOG

The Australian Shepherd is a very intelligent dog. Some people assume

that an intelligent dog will always know how to behave. More often than not, an intelligent dog will find different ways to do things, many times because he gets bored more easily. For example, if you teach the average dog to go get the morning newspaper, the dog will probably go get the paper every morning, doing the same thing day after day. The Aussie, however, will quickly get bored with that routine and will try and figure out how to add some ruffles and flourishes to the morning ritual. Perhaps he will pick up the paper by one end, or by the rubber band. Perhaps he will make three dashes around the car and then get the paper. Maybe he will play keep-away after getting the paper.

Because of the Aussie's drive to work and his high intelligence, obedience training is a necessity. This training will help establish (and reinforce) the dog-owner relationship and will give your Aussie a challenge. Dog sports are also good challenges, especially the active sports, such as Frisbee, agility and flyball.

AUSSIE ACTIVITY LEVEL

The Australian Shepherd is a fairly high-energy dog that requires daily exercise—strenuous daily exercise. A 2- or 3-mile walk around the neighborhood might be adequate exercise for a young puppy or an older dog, but cannot be considered exercise for a healthy adult. A good, fast run, a fast session of throwing the ball or a jog alongside a bicycle is more appropriate.

As mentioned earlier, the Australian Shepherd's drive to work can turn destructive if the dog doesn't have a job to do. The same thing can happen when the dog doesn't get enough

exercise. Many Aussies will pace, run the fences, bark, chew or try to escape from the yard when they are alone, bored and have an excess of energy. However, when your Aussie gets enough exercise on a daily basis, he will be healthier, happier and more relaxed, and destructiveness around the house and yard will be decreased.

Aussies are very active. Playing and exercising with your dog daily will prevent him from becoming restless.

HAIR, HAIR AND MORE HAIR!

Aussies shed. There is no way around it. That lush, thick silky coat does shed. If dog hair in the house bothers you, don't get an Aussie. Australian Shepherd owners deal with the problem in different ways. Some vacuum daily, others buy carpet that

Cleaning up after a shedding Aussie is a lot of work—but well worth it.

worst shedding times are spring and fall, depending upon the climate, but some shedding takes place all year-round. The easiest way to keep it under control is to brush the dog thoroughly every day. See Chapter 5, "Putting on the Dog" for more detail, but it is important to note shedding here because it affects how you live with your dog.

NEAT AND CLEAN

Other than shedding, Aussies are very clean dogs. Most housetrain very easily and will relieve themselves in one spot in the yard, often in a corner or up against a bush. Most will walk around a pile of feces, not wanting to even touch it. Aussies do not drool, and their personal habits are very clean. Their silky coat sheds dirt easily and even a muddy Aussie will be fairly clean after drying and a brushing.

matches the dog's coat, others pull up the carpet and put down tile. Living with a dog requires some compromises, and dealing with dog hair without complaining is one of them.

However, you can take measures to keep shedding under control. The

CHAPTER TWO

Homecoming

FIRST THINGS FIRST

Before you bring your Australian
Shepherd home, you will need some
supplies; you don't want to have to
make an emergency run to the store

at midnight because you forgot something. Most of these are basic neces-
sities for both the puppy and the
adopted adult.

Food

Obviously, you will need dog food. Find out what the puppy has been eating and get some of the same food. If you wish to switch to a different brand, do so over an extended period of time so your Australian Shepherd can adjust. Rapid changes in diet can result in an upset stomach and diarrhea.

Food and Water Dishes

You will need a bowl for food and a bowl for water. The food bowl can be just about anything; some people like plastic, others like ceramic or stainless steel. Whatever you use should be large enough to hold 4 to 6 cups of food and should be easy to clean. Change the water and clean the bowl daily. If your Australian Shepherd likes to splash in it, check it a couple times a day to make sure the dog doesn't go thirsty.

Leash and Collar

You will also need a collar and leash for your new Aussie. A buckle collar, either with a metal buckle or the plastic quick release closure, is good for both puppies and adult dogs. Adjustable collars are available that can be made larger as the puppy grows.

ID Tag

All puppies need some form of identification, even before receiving their rabies shots and being licensed. Most pet stores and veterinary offices have access to sources that make identification tags that can be attached to the puppy's collar. It is more important that the owner's name is on this tag than the dog's name.

An additional protection is to have your dog tattooed when she reaches maturity. Your social security number can be used for identification and listed with a tattoo registry for dogs. Another form of identification is a microchip that is actually implanted under the dog's skin. Should your dog be lost, a sensing device locates her. Tattoos and microchips are excellent forms of ID; however, the person who finds a dog may not know to look for a tattoo, and certainly would not know to look for a microchip. Consequently, a dog should wear an ID tag as well as a tattoo or microchip.

Crate

Your new Aussie will need a kennel crate to use as a bed, a place of refuge and a place for quiet time. This crate can be the plastic kind like airlines require, or it can be a heavy metal wire cage. The style is up to you, but the crate should be large enough for an adult Australian Shepherd to stand up, turn around and lay down in comfortably.

Dogs enjoy having a crate of their own for sleeping, eating and quiet time.

Toys

Fleece-covered shaptes, braided ropes and hard rubber balls are just a few Aussie favorites. As a puppy matures and gets her adult teeth, a variety of items made of hard nylon compounds in a variety of shapes can provide

9

Excessive chewing can be partially resolved by providing a puppy with her own chew toys.

PUPPY ESSENTIALS

To prepare yourself and your family for your puppy's homecoming, and to be sure your pup has what she needs, you should obtain the following:

Food and Water Bowls: One for each. We recommend stainless steel or heavy crockery—something solid but easy to clean.

Bed and/or Crate Pad: Something soft, washable and big enough for your soon-to-be-adult dog.

Crate: Make housetraining easier and provide a safe, secure den for your dog with a crate—it only looks like a cage to you!

Toys: As much fun to buy as they are for your pup to play with. Don't overwhelm your puppy with too many toys, though, especially the first few days she's home. And be sure to include something hollow you can stuff with goodies, like a Kong.

I.D. Tag: Inscribed with your name and phone number.

Collar: An adjustable buckle collar is best. Remember, your pup's going to grow fast!

Leash: Style is nice, but durability and your comfort while holding it count, too. You can't go wrong with leather for most dogs.

Grooming Supplies: The proper brushes, special shampoo, toenail clippers, a toothbrush and doggy toothpaste.

hours of chewing enjoyment. Anything given to a dog must be large enough that it cannot be swallowed.

PREPARING YOUR HOME

Prior to bringing home your Australian Shepherd, you will need to make sure your house is ready. First of all, set up the crate in your bedroom. This way your dog will spend six to eight hours close to you and can smell and hear you all night long. This is a great way to bond with the dog and reassure her as she adjusts to her new home. Also, if the puppy needs to go outside during the night, you will hear her whine and cry before she has an accident.

Next, decide where your dog will spend her days. If you are home all day, this is not as big of a problem as you can supervise the puppy when she's out and about. When you can't watch the pup, you can put her in her crate. However, if you work away from home, you will need a secure place for the dog to stay while you are gone. For example, a room such as a bathroom equipped with doggie bed, water, toys and a toilet.

If you will be leaving your Australian Shepherd outside, you might want to build a secure run or exercise area. Make sure the dog won't be able to climb or dig out of it and that other dogs, coyotes or predators can't get in. Your dog will need a house and shelter from the weather and an unspillable water bowl.

Puppyproofing Your Home

Next, you must make sure your house, yard and garage are safe for your new Australian Shepherd. In the house, crawl around on your hands and knees and look at things from a dog's viewpoint. Pick up or put away anything that looks even remotely interesting. Start teaching family members to close closet doors, pick up dirty clothes and put away shoes and slippers. With a young puppy or a new dog in the house, keeping temptation out of reach is imperative.

If your Australian Shepherd will have access to the garage, make sure all chemicals, paints and car parts are up high out of reach. Antifreeze especially is very poisonous and dogs seem to love the taste.

In the yard, look for possible escape routes—places where your dog could go under or over the fence. A pile of lumber or a rabbit hutch next to the fence could provide an easy

IDENTIFY YOUR DOG

It is a terrible thing to think about, but your dog could somehow, someday, get lost or stolen. For safety's sake, every dog should wear a buckle collar with an identification tag. A tag is the first thing a stranger will look for on a lost dog. Inscribe the tag with your name and phone number.

There are two ways to permanently identify your dog. The first is a tattoo, placed on the inside of your dog's thigh. The tattoo should be your social security number or your dog's AKC registration number. The second is a microchip, a rice-sized pellet that is inserted under the dog's skin at the base of the neck between the shoulder blades. When a scanner is passed over the dog, it will beep, notifying the person that the dog has a chip. The scanner will then show a code, identifying the dog.

escape route. A drainage ditch running under the fence could do the same thing. Again, try to look at your yard from the dog's point of view. Put away garden tools, fertilizers, pesticides and pool supplies. Check the list of poisonous plants to make sure your landscaping and potted plants are safe just in case your dog does try to sample them.

When you must leave your Aussies unsupervised, designate an area in your home where they can be safe and secure.

AN AUSTRALIAN SHEPHERD IN THE HOUSE

Setting Up a Schedule

Dogs are creatures of habit and thrive on a regular routine that doesn't vary too much from day to day. Puppies, especially, need a routine. At 8 weeks of age, puppies sleep a lot. Your puppy will eat, relieve herself, play and sleep, and a couple of hours later will repeat the whole cycle. However, as she gets older, she will gradually sleep less and play more. As she learns and develops bowel and bladder control, she will go longer

Australian Shepherds are very people-oriented dogs and must spend time with their owners.

periods between needing to relieve herself—from every couple of hours to every three or four hours. Your household routine will dictate what your dog's schedule will look like.

Quality Time Is a Must

Your dog should be inside with you when you are home and should be next to your bed at night. In addition, you will need to make time to play with your dog, train her and make sure that she gets enough exercise.

Crate Training

Adding a puppy to your household can be a wonderful experience, but it can sour quickly if the puppy is ruining your carpets and chewing up your shoes. There is a training tool that can help—a crate.

A crate allows you to use the dog's natural denning instincts; the instinct that makes dogs curl up behind the chair or under a table when they nap. Puppies also have a natural instinct not to soil or relieve themselves in the place where they sleep. A crate helps housetrain a puppy by using that instinct.

Introduce the crate by opening the door and tossing a treat or toy

HOUSEHOLD DANGERS

Curious puppies and inquisitive dogs get into trouble not because they are bad, but simply because they want to investigate the world around them. It's our job to protect our dogs from harmful substances, like the following:

In the Garage

antifreeze

garden supplies, like snail and slug bait, pesticides, fertilizers, mouse and rat poisons

In the House

cleaners, especially pine oil

perfumes, colognes, aftershaves

medications, vitamins

office and craft supplies

electric cords

chicken or turkey bones

chocolate, onions

some house and garden plants, like ivy, oleander and poinsettia

13

inside. Allow the puppy to come and go as she pleases, and to investigate the crate. When she is going in after the treat or toy, give her a treat and close the door. Leave the door closed for a few minutes and then let the

Crate training your Australian Shepherd at an early age will teach her to enjoy settling down in her own special place.

puppy out if, and only if, the puppy is being quiet. If the puppy is throwing a temper tantrum, don't let her out. If you do, you will have taught your puppy that a temper tantrum works.

Put the puppy in her crate when you are home and can't supervise her or when you are busy, such as eating a meal. Put the puppy in the crate when she is overstimulated—time

outs are good for puppies, too. And of course, put the puppy in her crate for the night.

Never leave the puppy in the crate longer than four hours except at night when the crate is next to your bed. It takes a while for the puppy to develop good bowel and bladder control and you need to be able to let the puppy out when it is time.

CHAPTER THREE

To Good Health

The strongest body and soundest genetic background will not help a dog lead a healthy life unless he receives regular attention from his owner. Dogs are susceptible to infection, parasites and diseases for which they have no natural immunity. It is up to us to take preventative measures to make sure that none of these interferes with our dog's health. It may help to think of the upkeep of a dog's health in relation to the calendar. Certain things need to be done on a weekly, monthly and annual basis.

PREVENTIVE HEALTH CARE

Weekly grooming can be the single best monitor of a dog's overall health.

The actual condition of the coat and skin and the "feel" of the body can indicate good health or potential

PREVENTIVE CARE PAYS

Using common sense, paying attention to your dog and working with your veterinarian, you can minimize health risks and problems. Use vet-recommended flea, tick and heartworm preventive medications; feed a nutritious diet appropriate for your dog's size, age and activity level; give your dog sufficient exercise and regular grooming; train and socialize your dog; keep current on your dog's shots; and enjoy all the years you have with your friend.

Run your hands over your dog to feel for any injuries. problems. Grooming will help you discover small lumps on or under the skin in the early stages before they become large enough to be seen without close examination.

Tick Control

As you examine your dog, check also for ticks that may have lodged in his skin, particularly around the ears or in the hair at the base of the ear, the armpits or around the genitals. If you find a tick, which is a small insect about the size of a pencil eraser when engorged with blood, smear it with petroleum jelly. As the tick suffocates, it will back out and you can then grab it with tweezers and kill it. If the tick doesn't back out, grab

it with tweezers and gently pull it out, twisting very gently. Don't just grab and pull or the tick's head may remain in the skin, causing an infection or abscess for which veterinary treatment may be required.

A word of caution: Don't use your fingers or fingernails to pull out ticks. Ticks can carry a number of diseases, including Lyme disease, Rocky Mountain spotted fever and others, all of which can be very serious.

17

Proper Ear Care

Another weekly job is cleaning the ears. Many times an ear problem is evident if a dog scratches his ears or shakes his head frequently. Clean ears are less likely to develop problems, and if something does occur, it will be spotted and it can be treated easily. If a dog's ears are very dirty and seem to need cleaning on a daily basis, it is a good indication that something else is going on in the ears besides ordinary dirt and the normal accumulation of earwax. A visit to the veterinarian may indicate a situation that needs special attention.

Keeping Eyes Clear

An Australian Shepherd's eyes rarely need special attention. A small

amount of matter in the corner of the eye is normal, as is a bit of "tearing."

Australian Shepherds with eyelashes that turn inward and rub

Aussies love the outdoors, so be sure to check frequently for fleas and ticks.

Use tweezers to remove ticks from your dog.

FLEAS AND TICKS

There are so many safe, effective products available now to combat fleas and ticks that—thankfully—they are less of a problem. Prevention is key, however. Ask your veterinarian about starting your puppy on a flea/tick repellent right away. With this, regular grooming and environmental controls, your dog and your home should stay pest-free. Without this attention, you risk infesting your dog and your home, and you're in for an ugly and costly battle to clear up the problem.

against the eye itself often exhibit more tearing than normal due to the irritation to the eyes. These eyelashes can be surgically removed if it appears to be a problem, but are often ignored.

Excessive tearing can be an indication that a tear duct is blocked. This, too, can be corrected by a simple surgical procedure. Eye discharge that is thicker and mucous-like in consistency is often a sign of some type of eye infection or actual injury to the eye. This can be verified by a veterinarian, who will provide a topical ointment to place in the corner of the eye. Most minor eye injuries heal quickly if proper action is taken.

VACCINES

The DHL vaccine, which protects a dog from distemper, hepatitis and leptospirosis, is given for the first time at about 7 weeks of age, followed by one or two boosters several weeks

18

Clean your Aussie's ears weekly and have them examined regularly by a veterinarian to detect problems.

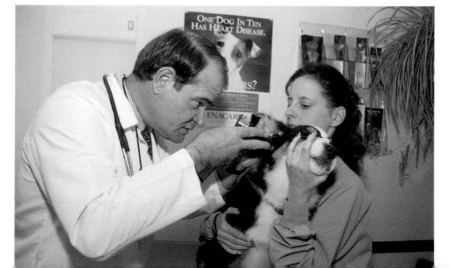

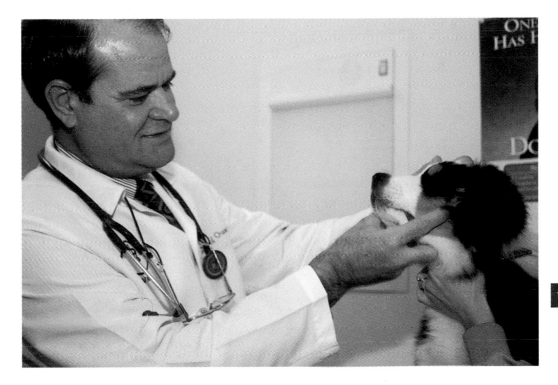

apart. After this, a dog should be vaccinated every year throughout his life.

Since the mid-1970s, parvovirus and coronavirus have been the cause of death for thousands of dogs. Puppies and older dogs are most frequently affected by these illnesses. Fortunately, vaccines for these are now routinely given on a yearly basis in combination with the DHLPP shot.

Kennel cough, though rarely dangerous in a healthy dog that receives proper treatment, can be annoying. It can be picked up anywhere that large numbers of dogs congregate, such as veterinary clinics, grooming shops, boarding kennels, obedience classes and dog shows. The Bordatella vaccine, given twice a year, will protect a dog from getting most strains of kennel cough. It is often not routinely given, so it may be necessary to request it.

INTERNAL PARASITES

While the exterior part of a dog's body hosts fleas and ticks, the inside

This Aussie sits patiently as the veterinarian examines his eyes and checks for irritants.

YOUR PUPPY'S VACCINES

Vaccines are given to prevent your dog from getting infectious diseases like canine distemper or rabies. Vaccines are the ultimate preventive medicine: They're given before your dog ever gets the disease so as to protect him from the disease. That's why it is necessary for your dog to be vaccinated routinely. Puppy vaccines start at 8 weeks of age for the five-in-one DHLPP vaccine and are given every three to four weeks until the puppy is 16 months old. Your veterinarian will put your puppy on a proper schedule and will remind you when to bring in your dog for shots.

All dogs need vaccinations to protect them from common deadly diseases.

of the body is commonly inhabited by a variety of parasites. Most of these are in the worm family. Tapeworms, roundworms, whipworms, hookworms and heartworm all plague dogs. There are also several types of protozoa, mainly *coccidia* and *giardia*, that cause problems.

Tapeworm

The common tapeworm is acquired by a dog eating infected fleas or lice. Normally one is not aware that a healthy dog even has tapeworms. The only clues may be a dull coat, a loss of weight despite a good appetite or occasional gastrointestinal problems. Confirmation is the presence of worm segments in the stool. These appear as small, pinkish-white, flattened rectangular-shaped pieces. When dry, they look like rice. If segments are not present, diagnosis can be made by the discovery of eggs when a stool sample is examined under a microscope. Ridding a dog temporarily of tapeworm is easy with a worming medicine prescribed by a veterinarian. Over-the-counter wormers are not effective for tapeworms and may be dangerous. Long-term tapeworm control is not possible unless the flea situation is also handled.

Roundworm

Ascarids are the most common roundworm (nematode) found in dogs. Adult dogs that have roundworms

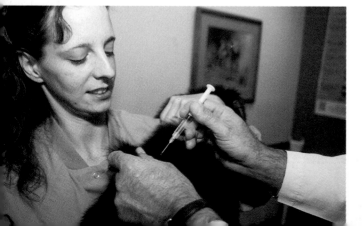

rarely exhibit any symptoms that would indicate the worm is in their body. These worms are cylindrical in shape and may be as long as 4 to 5 inches. They do pose a real danger to puppies, where they are usually passed from the mother through the uterus to the unborn puppies.

It is wise to assume that all puppies have roundworms. In heavy infestations they will actually appear in the puppy stools, though their presence is best diagnosed by a stool sample. Treatment is easy and can begin as early as 2 weeks of age and is administered every two weeks thereafter until eggs no longer appear in a stool sample or dead worms are not found in the stool following treatment. Severely infected puppies can die from roundworm infestation. Again, the worming medication should be obtained through a veterinarian.

Hookworm

Hookworm is usually found in warmer climates and infestation is generally from ingestion of larvae from the ground or penetration of the skin by larvae. Hookworms can cause anemia, diarrhea and emaciation. As these

Proper care, regular vaccinations, and stool checks and preventive medications for such things as heartworm will help ensure your dog's health.

21

worms are very tiny and not visible to the eye, their diagnosis must be made by a veterinarian.

Whipworm

Whipworms live in the large intestine and cause few if any symptoms. Dogs usually become infected when they ingest larvae in contaminated soil. Again, diagnosis and treatment should all be done by a veterinarian. One of the easiest ways to control these parasites is by picking up stools on a daily basis. This will help prevent the soil from becoming infested.

The protozoa can be trickier to diagnose and treat. Coccidiosis and giardia are the most common, and primarily affect young puppies. They are generally associated with over-crowded, unsanitary conditions and can be acquired from the mother (if she is a carrier), the premises them-selves (soil) or even water, especially rural puddles and streams.

The most common symptom of protozoan infection is mucous-like, blood-tinged feces. It is only with freshly collected samples that diag-nosis of this condition can be made. With coccidiosis, besides diarrhea, the puppies will appear listless and lose their appetites. Puppies often

harbor the protozoa and show no symptoms unless placed under stress. Consequently, often a puppy will not become ill until he enters his new home. Once diagnosed, treatment is quick and effective and the puppy returns to normal almost immediately.

Heartworm

The most serious of the common internal parasites is the heartworm. A dog that is bitten by a mosquito infected with the heartworm *micro-filaria* (larvae) will develop worms that are 6 to 12 inches long. As these worms mature, they take up residence in the dog's heart.

The symptoms of heartworm may include coughing, tiring easily, diffi-culty breathing and weight loss. Heart failure and liver disease may eventu-ally result. Verification of heartworm infection is done by drawing blood and screening for the microfilaria.

In areas where heartworm is a risk, it is best to place a dog on a pre-ventative, usually a pill given once a month.

At least once a year a dog should have a full veterinary examination. The overall condition of the dog can be observed and a blood sample can be collected for a complete yearly screening. This way the dog's thyroid function can be tested, and the job the dog's organs are doing can be monitored. If there are any problems, this form of testing can spot trouble areas while they are easily treatable.

SPAYING/NEUTERING

Spaying a female dog or neutering a male is another way to make sure they lead long and healthy lives. Females spayed at a young age have almost no risk of developing mammary tumors or reproductive problems. Neutering a male is an excellent solution to dog aggression and also removes the chances of testicular cancer.

Female Australian Shepherds usually experience their first heat cycle somewhere between 6 months and 1 year of age. Unless spayed they will continue to come into heat on a regular cycle. The length of time between heats varies, with anything from every six months to a year being normal.

There is absolutely no benefit to a female having a first season before being spayed, nor in letting her have a litter. The decision to breed any dog should never be taken lightly. The obvious considerations are whether he or she is a good physical specimen

ADVANTAGES OF SPAY/NEUTER

The greatest advantage of spaying (for females) or neutering (for males) your dog is that you are guaranteed your dog will not produce puppies. There are too many puppies already available for too few homes. There are other advantages as well.

Advantages of Spaying

No messy heats.

No "suitors" howling at your windows or waiting in your yard.

No risk of pyometra (disease of the uterus) and decreased incidences of mammary cancer.

Advantages of Neutering

Decreased incidences of fighting, but does not affect the dog's personality.

Decreased roaming in search of bitches in season.

Decreased incidences of many urogenital diseases.

of the breed and has a sound temperament. There are several genetic problems that are common to Australian Shepherds, such as eye defects, hip dysplasia and cancer. Responsible breeders screen for these prior to making breeding decisions.

23

Finding suitable homes for puppies is another serious consideration. Due to their popularity, many people are attracted to Australian Shepherds and seek puppies without realizing the drawbacks of the breed.

Owning a dog is a lifetime commitment to that animal. There are so many unwanted dogs—and yes, even unwanted Australian Shepherds—that people must be absolutely sure that they are not just adding to the pet over-population problem. When breeding a litter of puppies, it is more likely that you will lose more than

Get to know your Australian Shepherd's eating habits—if he starts missing meals he may be ill.

you will make, when time, effort, equipment and veterinary costs are factored in.

COMMON PROBLEMS

Not Eating or Vomiting

One of the surest signs that an Australian Shepherd may be ill is if he does not eat. That is why it is important to know your dog's eating habits. For most dogs, one missed meal under normal conditions is not cause for alarm, but more than that and it is time to take your dog to the veterinarian to search for reasons. The vital signs should be checked and gums examined. Normally a dog's gums are pink; if ill they will be pale and gray.

There are many reasons why dogs vomit, and many of them are not cause for alarm. You should be concerned, however, when your dog vomits frequently over the period of a day. If the vomiting is associated with diarrhea, elevated temperature and lethargy, the cause is most likely a virus. The dog should receive supportive veterinary treatment if recovery is to proceed quickly. Vomiting that is not associated with other symptoms is often an indication of an intestinal blockage. Rocks, toys and clothing will lodge in a dog's intestine, preventing the normal passage of digested foods and liquids.

If a blockage is suspected, the first thing to do is an x-ray of the stomach and intestinal region. Sometimes objects will pass on their own, but usually surgical removal of the object is necessary.

Diarrhea

Diarrhea is characterized as very loose to watery stools that a dog has difficulty controlling. It can be caused by anything as simple as changing diet, eating too much food, eating rich human food or having internal parasites.

First try to locate the source of the problem and remove it from the dog's access. Immediate relief is usually available by giving the dog an intestinal relief medication such as Kaopectate or Pepto-Bismol. Use the same amount per weight as for humans. Take the dog off his food for a day to allow the intestines to rest, then feed meals of cooked rice with bland ingredients added. Gradually add the dog's regular food back into his diet.

If diarrhea is bloody or has a more offensive odor than might be expected

WHEN TO CALL THE VETERINARIAN

In any emergency situation, you should call your veterinarian immediately. Try to stay calm when you call, and give the vet or the assistant as much information as possible before you leave for the clinic. That way, the staff will be able to take immediate, specific action when you arrive. Emergencies include:

- Bleeding or deep wounds
- Hyperthermia (overheating)
- Shock
- Dehydration
- Abdominal pain
- Burns
- Fits
- Unconsciousness
- Broken bones
- Paralysis

Call your veterinarian if you suspect any health troubles.

and is combined with vomiting and fever, it is most likely a virus and requires immediate veterinary attention. If worms are suspected as the cause, a stool sample should be examined by a veterinarian and treatment to rid the dog of the parasite should follow when the dog is back to normal. If allergies are suspected, a series of tests can be given to find the cause. This is especially likely if after recovery and no other evidence of a cause exists, a dog returns to his former diet and the diarrhea recurs.

Dehydration

To test your dog for dehydration, take some skin between your thumb and forefinger and lift the skin upward

Some of the many household substances harmful to your dog.

gently. If the skin does not go back to its original position quickly, the Australian Shepherd may be suffering from dehydration. Consult your veterinarian immediately.

Poisoning

Vomiting, breathing with difficulty, diarrhea, cries of pain and abnormal body or breath odor are all signs that your pet may have ingested some poisonous substance. Poisons can also be inhaled, absorbed through the skin or injected into the skin, as in the case of a snakebite. Poisons require professional help without delay! Call the National Animal Poison Control Center hot line at (900) 680-0000. The call will be charged to your phone—$20.00 for the first five minutes and $2.95 for each additional minute.

POISON ALERT

If your dog has ingested a potentially poisonous substance, waste no time. Call the National Animal Poison Control Center hot line:

(800) 548-2423 ($30 per case) or

(900) 680-0000 ($20 first five minutes; $2.95 each additional minute)

Broken Bones

If your dog breaks a bone, immobilize the limb very carefully, and seek veterinary help right away. If you suspect a spinal injury, place the dog on a board very slowly and carefully tie him securely to the board before immediately transporting him to the veterinarian.

Scratches and Cuts

Minor skin irritations, such as scratches, can usually be cured by using an over-the-counter antibiotic cream or ointment. For minor skin problems, many ointments suitable for a baby work well on an Australian Shepherd.

Heatstroke

Heatstroke can quickly lead to death. *Never* leave your dog in a car, even with the windows open, even on a cloudy day with the car under the shade of a tree. Heat builds up quickly; your dog could die in a matter of minutes. Do not leave your Australian Shepherd outside on a hot day especially if no shade or water is provided.

Heatstroke symptoms include collapse, high fever, diarrhea, vomiting, excessive panting and grayish lips. If you notice these symptoms, you need to cool the animal immediately. Try to reduce the body temperature with towels soaked in cold water; massage the body and legs very gently. Fanning the dog may help. If the dog will drink cool water, let him. If he will not drink, wipe the inside of his mouth with cool water. Get the dog to the nearest veterinary hospital. Do not delay!

Make a temporary splint by wrapping the leg in firm casing, then bandaging it.

Bee Stings

Bee stings are painful and may cause an allergic reaction. Symptoms may be swelling around the bite and difficulty breathing. Severe allergic reaction could lead to death. If a stinger is present, remove it. Clean the bitten area thoroughly with alcohol; apply a cold compress to reduce swelling and itching and an anti-inflammatory ointment or cream medication. Seek medical help.

Choking

Puppies are curious creatures and will naturally chew anything they can get into their mouths, be it a bone, a twig,

Applying abdominal thrusts can save a choking dog.

27

WHAT'S WRONG WITH MY DOG?

We've listed some common conditions of health problems and their possible causes. If any of the following conditions appear serious or persist for more than 24 hours, make an appointment to see your veterinarian immediately.

CONDITIONS	POSSIBLE CAUSES
DIARRHEA	Intestinal upset, typically caused by eating something bad or over-eating. Can also be a viral infection, a bad case of nerves or anxiety or a parasite infection. If you see blood in the feces, get to the vet right away.
VOMITING/RETCHING	Dogs regurgitate fairly regularly (bitches for their young), whenever something upsets their stomachs, or even out of excitement or anxiety. Often dogs eat grass, which, because it's indigestible in its pure form, irritates their stomachs and causes them to vomit. Getting a good look at *what* your dog vomited can better indicate what's causing it.
COUGHING	Obstruction in the throat; virus (kennel cough); roundworm infestation; congestive heart failure.
RUNNY NOSE	Because dogs don't catch colds like people, a runny nose is a sign of congestion or irritation.
LOSS OF APPETITE	Because most dogs are hearty and regular eaters, a loss of appetite can be your first and most accurate sign of a serious problem.
LOSS OF ENERGY (LETHARGY)	Any number of things could be slowing down your dog, from an infection to internal tumors to overexercise—even overeating.

stones, tiny toys, string or any number of things. These can get caught in the teeth or, worse, lodged in the throat and may finally rest in the stomach or intestines. Symptoms may be drooling, pawing at the mouth, gagging, difficulty breathing, blue tongue or mouth, difficulty swallowing and bloody vomit. If the foreign object can be seen and you can remove it easily, do so. If you can't remove it yourself, use the

CONDITIONS	POSSIBLE CAUSES
STINKY BREATH	Imagine if you never brushed your teeth! Foul-smelling breath indicates plaque and tartar buildup that could possibly have caused infection. Start brushing your dog's teeth.
LIMPING	This could be caused by something as simple as a hurt or bruised pad, to something as complicated as hip dysplasia, torn ligaments or broken bones.
CONSTANT ITCHING	Probably due to fleas, mites or an allergic reaction to food or environment (your vet will need to help you determine what your dog's allergic to).
RED, INFLAMED, ITCHY SPOTS	Often referred to as "hot spots," these are particularly common on coated breeds. They're caused by a bacterial infection that gets aggravated as the dog licks and bites at the spot.
BALD SPOTS	These are the result of excessive itching or biting at the skin so that the hair follicles are damaged; excessively dry skin; mange; calluses; and even infections. You need to determine what the underlying cause is.
STINKY EARS/HEAD SHAKING	Take a look under your dog's ear flap. Do you see brown, waxy buildup? Clean the ears with something soft and a special cleaner, and don't use cotton swabs or go too deep into the ear canal.
UNUSUAL LUMPS	Could be fatty tissue, could be something serious (infection, trauma, tumor). Don't wait to find out.

Heimlich maneuver. Place your dog on his side and, using both hands palms down, apply quick thrusts to the abdomen, just below the dog's last rib. If your dog won't lie down, grasp either side of the end of the rib cage and squeeze in short thrusts. Make a sharp enough movement to cause the air in the lungs to force the object out. If the cause cannot be found or removed, then professional help is needed.

Bleeding

For open wounds, try to stop the bleeding by applying pressure to the wound for five minutes using a sterile bandage. If bleeding has not stopped after this time, continue the pressure. Do not remove the pad if it sticks to the wound because more serious injury could result. Just place a new sterile bandage over the first, and apply a little more pressure to stop the bleeding. This procedure will usually be successful. Take the dog to the medical center for treatment, especially if the bleeding cannot be controlled rapidly.

If bleeding cannot be stopped with pressure, try pressing on the upper inside of the effected leg; for tail bleeding, press on the underside of the tail at its base. Do not attempt to stop the bleeding with a tourniquet unless the bleeding is profuse and cannot be stopped any other way. A tourniquet must be tight; consequently, it cannot be left on for a long time because it will stop the circulation. It could be more dangerous than the bleeding!

Burns

Do not put creams or oils on a burn. Cool water can be used to carefully wash the burn area. Transport to the veterinary clinic immediately.

Your Australian Shepherd cannot take care of himself. When you took this dog home, you assumed the responsibility of caring for him. This means not just making sure he is fed and brushed, but also checking his nails, making sure vaccinations are up-to-date and getting him to the veterinarian when necessary. The easiest way to make sure your dog is well cared for is to set up a routine and follow it each and every day without fail.

HEALTH PROBLEMS IN THE AUSTRALIAN SHEPHERD

AUTOIMMUNE PROBLEMS—The dog's immune system protects him from disease; when a virus or bacteria enters the body, white blood cells are triggered to combat them. In a dog with an immune system problem, the body will not produce these white blood cells, or with an autoimmune problem, it will begin producing white blood cells to attack itself. Although the causes of autoimmune disease can vary, some researchers feel that there is a genetic predisposition toward it. Dogs with any autoimmune disease should not be used for breeding.

BLOAT—Bloat is the acute dilation of the stomach, caused when the stomach fills with gas and air and as a result, swells. This swelling prevents the dog from vomiting or passing gas, and as a result, the pressure builds, cutting off blood from the heart and to other parts of the body. This causes shock or heart failure, both of which can cause death. Bloat can also cause torsion, where the stomach turns on its long axis, again causing death.

The first symptoms of bloat are obvious. The dog will be pacing or panting, showing signs of distress. The dog's sides will begin to distend. To be successful, treatment should begin at once—there is no time to fool around. If the pressure is not immediately relieved, death can follow within an hour.

To prevent bloat, do not allow your Australian Shepherd to drink large quantities of water after exercising or after eating. Feed two smaller meals each day instead of one large meal and limit exercise after eating until a couple hours have passed. Feed a good quality food, preferably one that does not expand significantly when wet and that does not produce large quantities of gas.

CANCER—Unfortunately, some Australian Shepherd lineages seem to be prone to cancer. Cancer in dogs, just as in people, is not one disease, but a variety of diseases. Although research is continuing, it is unknown how or why some cells go on a rampage and become cancerous. When you examine your Australian Shepherd each day, be aware of any lumps or bumps you might feel, especially as your dog is growing older. Your veterinarian can biopsy any suspicious lump; if it is cancer, it can often be removed. Early removal has the best chance of success. Unfortunately, cancer is often fatal.

EYE DEFECTS—Aussies have been known to have some eye defects. There are several different types of

Learning about the specific health problems of the Australian Shepherd breed will help you better care for your dog.

31

eye defects found. Aussies should have an eye screening as early as 8 weeks of age, prior to being sold or going to a new home. Every Aussie, especially those used in a breeding program, should have his eyes examined each year.

HIP DYSPLASIA—Hip Dysplasia (HD) is a disease of the coxofemoral joint; to put it simply, it is a failure of the head of the femur (thigh bone) to fit into the acetabulum (hip socket). HD is not simply caused by poorly formed or positioned bones; many researchers feel that the muscles and tendons in the leg and hip may also play a part in the disease.

HD is considered to be a polygenic inherited disorder, which means that many factors come into play. Many different genes may lead to the disease, not just one. Also, environmental factors may lead to HD, including nutrition and exercise, although the part that environmental factors play in the disease is highly debated among experts.

HD can cause a wide range of problems, from mild lameness to movement irregularities to crippling

pain. Dogs with HD must often limit their activities, may need corrective surgery or may even need to be put to sleep because of the pain.

PANOSTEITIS—This disease causes lameness and pain in young, rapidly growing puppies, usually between the ages of 6 and 14 months, although it is occasionally seen in dogs up to 18 months of age. The lameness usually affects one leg at a time and can sporadically move from one leg to another. Some veterinarians prescribe aspirin to relieve the pain and most suggest the dog be kept quiet.

THYROID DISEASE—The thyroid gland produces hormones which govern or affect a number of different bodily functions. A dog with a thyroid that is producing less hormones than it should may show symptoms ranging from infertility to dry, dull coat and flaky skin, to running eyes or even difficulty walking. Thyroid problems can be diagnosed with a blood test and medication can usually relieve the symptoms fairly rapidly. In most cases, the dog will have to remain on the medication for life.

CHAPTER FOUR

Positively Nutritious

The nutritional needs of a dog will change throughout her lifetime. It is necessary to be aware of these changes not only for proper initial growth to occur, but also so your dog can lead a healthy life for many years.

Before bringing your puppy home, ask the breeder for the puppy's feeding schedule and information about what and how much she is used to eating. Maintain this regimen for at least the first few days before gradually changing to a schedule that is more in line with your family's lifestyle. The breeder may supply you with a small quantity of the food the puppy has been eating. Use this, or have your own supply of the same food ready when you bring home your puppy.

After the puppy has been with you for three days and has become acclimated to her new environment, you can begin a gradual food change. Add a portion of the new food to the usual food. Add a little more of the new food each day until it has entirely replaced the previous diet. This gradual change will prevent an upset stomach and diarrhea. The total amount of food to be fed at each meal will remain the same at this stage of the puppy's life.

LIFE-STAGE FEEDING

Puppies and adolescent dogs require a much higher intake of protein, calories and nutrients than adult dogs due to the demands of their rapidly developing bodies. Most commercial brands of dry kibble meet these requirements and are well balanced for proper growth. The majority of puppy foods now available are so carefully planned that it is unwise to attempt to add anything other than water to them.

The major ingredients of most dry dog foods are chicken, beef or lamb by-products and corn, wheat or rice. The higher the meat content, the higher the protein percentage, palatability and digestibility of the food. Protein percentages in puppy food are

Playful puppies require more calories and protein in their diets than do adult dogs.

usually between 25 and 40 percent. There are many advantages of dry foods over semimoist and canned dog foods for puppies and normal, healthy adult Australian Shepherds.

It is best to feed meals that are primarily dry food because the chewing action involved in eating a dry food is better for the health of the teeth and gums. Dry food is also less expensive than canned food of equal quality.

Dogs whose diets are based on canned or soft foods have a greater likelihood of developing calcium deposits and gum disease. Canned or semimoist foods do serve certain functions, however. As a supplement to dry dog food, in small portions, canned or semimoist foods can be useful to stimulate appetites and aid in weight gain. But unless very

GROWTH STAGE FOODS

Once upon a time, there was puppy food and there was adult dog food. Now there are foods for puppies, young adults/active dogs, less active dogs and senior citizens. What's the difference between these foods? They vary by the amounts of nutrients they provide for the dog's growth stage/activity level.

Less active dogs don't need as much protein or fat as growing, active dogs; senior dogs don't need some of the nutrients vital to puppies. By feeding a high-quality food that's appropriate for your dog's age and activity level, you're benefiting your dog and yourself. Feed too much protein to a couch potato and she'll have energy to spare, which means a few more trips around the block will be needed to burn it off. Feed an adult diet to a puppy, and risk growth and development abnormalities that could affect her for a lifetime.

35

Feeding your Australian Shepherd dry food and crunchy treats helps keep her teeth and gums healthy.

How Many Meals a Day?

Individual dogs vary in how much they should eat to maintain a desired body weight—not too fat, but not too thin. Puppies need several meals a day, while older dogs may need only one. Determine how much food keeps your adult dog looking and feeling her best. Then decide how many meals you want to feed with that amount. Like us, most dogs love to eat, and offering two meals a day is more enjoyable for them. If you're worried about overfeeding, make sure you measure correctly and abstain from adding tidbits to the meals.

Whether you feed one or two meals, only leave your dog's food out for the amount of time it takes her to eat it—ten minutes, for example. Free-feeding (when food is available any time) and leisurely meals encourage picky eating. Don't worry if your dog doesn't finish all her dinner in the allotted time. She'll learn she should.

special conditions exist, they are not the best way for a dog to meet her food needs.

What's Best for Your Australian Shepherd

The Australian Shepherd has a wonderful appetite, and it is a rare Australian Shepherd who is a picky eater.

When people worry that their pet's diet is too boring, they are projecting their own feelings into a situation that is perfectly fine with the Australian Shepherd. Our concern should be finding a food that is convenient to feed, is completely balanced so that no supplements are necessary, is nutrient-dense so that less food is consumed and therefore less stool volume is generated, and is reasonably priced so that we don't have to re-structure our family grocery budget.

Different Dogs Need Different Diets

There has been considerable research over the past few years to suggest that nutrient requirements change according to age, condition, activity level, gestation, lactation and so on, and this only makes sense on an intuitive level. A dog that runs hundreds of miles a week hunting is going to burn more calories than an Australian Shepherd couch potato.

While the protein requirements may not change that much, the energy difference must come either from additional carbohydrates or from fat. Fat has more calories on a dry-weight basis than either protein or carbohydrates, so it is the logical choice for supplementing the diets of hardworking animals.

Advances in feed manufacturing techniques have made it possible to incorporate higher levels of fat into extruded dog foods than in the past, thereby eliminating the need for the dog owner to add it on after the fact, which used to throw the correct nutritional proportions out of balance.

HOW MUCH TO FEED?

If you take the recommendation of the breeder in selecting the food, keep in mind that the amounts they feed are based on the activity

FOOD ALLERGIES

If your puppy or dog seems to itch all the time for no apparent reason, she could be allergic to one or more ingredients in her food. This is not uncommon, and it's why many foods contain lamb and rice instead of beef, wheat or soy. Have your dog tested by your veterinarian, and be patient while you strive to identify and eliminate the allergens from your dog's food (or environment).

levels of their dogs in their geographical area. Similarly, the recommended feeding quantities as they appear on the bag are guidelines. Some Australian Shepherds will get fat on 1 cup of premium food

You can learn what and how much to feed your Aussie by her activity level, age and condition.

37

HOW TO READ
A DOG FOOD LABEL

With so many choices on the market, how can you be sure you are feeding the right food to your dog? The information is all there on the label—if you know what you're looking for.

Look for the nutritional claim right up top. Is the food "100 percent nutritionally complete"? If so, it's for nearly all life stages; "growth and maintenance," on the other hand, is for early development; puppy foods are marked as such, as are foods for senior dogs.

Ingredients are listed in descending order by weight. The first three or four ingredients will tell you the bulk of what the food contains. Look for the highest-quality ingredients, like meats and grains, to be among them.

The Guaranteed Analysis tells you what levels of protein, fat, fiber and moisture are in the food, in that order. While these numbers are meaningful, they won't tell you much about the quality of the food. Nutritional value is in the dry matter, not the moisture content.

In many ways, seeing is believing. If your dog has bright eyes, a shiny coat, a good appetite and a good energy level, chances are her diet's fine. Your dog's breeder and your veterinarian are good sources of advice if you're still confused.

a day, and another might require twice that just to keep her ribs from showing. This means you will have to use your own judgment after getting input from the vet, breeder and feed store.

A well-fed Australian Shepherd will always be a *bit* hungry, so that is not a clue as to the proper amount to feed. The rule of thumb as to whether your Australian Shepherd is the correct weight is that you should be able to feel her ribs but not see them. If she is free of parasites and kept reasonably clean, there should be a "bloom" on her coat that comes with just the right amount of subcutaneous fat.

Should you feed the meal wet or dry? There are pluses and minuses to each method, and you will have to determine what works best for you and your Australian Shepherd. Feeding wet usually means either moistening or soaking the dry food in warm water or broth for a few minutes. This method is recommended for young puppies, whose dentition may not be up to crunching down their meals easily. Advocates of wet feeding believe it results in less bloating. It may also increase palatability and digestibility—considerations more important for puppies than for adults.

Dry feeding requires no time delay and may help slow down a dog who would otherwise gulp down her food. It may also be better for your pet's dental health. Also, on those rare occasions when your pet doesn't immediately clean her plate, you needn't be concerned with spoilage.

Keep Your Australian Shepherd Slim

Finally, remember that obesity will shorten your Australian Shepherd's life span, increase the likelihood of health problems and in general reduce her quality of life.

TO SUPPLEMENT OR NOT TO SUPPLEMENT

If you're feeding your dog a diet that's correct for her developmental stage and she's alert, healthy looking and neither over- nor underweight, you don't need to add supplements. These include table scraps as well as vitamins and minerals. In fact, unless you are a nutrition expert, using food supplements can actually hurt a growing puppy. For example, mixing too much calcium into your dog's food can lead to musculoskeletal disorders. Educating yourself about the quantity of vitamins and minerals your dog needs to be healthy will help you determine what needs to be supplemented. If you have any concerns about the nutritional quality of the food you're feeding, discuss them with your veterinarian.

39

You should be able to feel (but not see) the ribs of a well-fed, fit Australian Shepherd.

TYPES OF FOOD/TREATS

There are three types of commercially available dog food—dry, canned and semimoist—and a huge assortment of treats (lucky dogs!) to feed your dog. Which should you choose?

Dry and canned foods contain similar ingredients. The primary difference between them is their moisture content. The moisture is not just water. It's blood and broth, too, the very things that dogs adore. So while canned food is more palatable, dry food is more economical, convenient and effective in controlling tartar buildup. Most owners feed a 25 percent canned/75 percent dry diet to give their dogs the benefit of both. Just be sure your dog is getting the nutrition she needs (you and your veterinarian can determine this).

Semimoist foods have the flavor dogs love and the convenience owners want. However, they tend to contain excessive amounts of artificial colors and preservatives.

Dog treats come in every size, shape and flavor imaginable, from organic cookies shaped like postmen to beefy chew sticks. Dogs seem to love them all, so enjoy the variety. Just be sure not to overindulge your dog. Factor treats into her regular meal sizes.

The occasional biscuit, bit of meat or cooked egg can be given as a special treat, but on the whole fewer treats will result in a happier, healthier Australian Shepherd.

CHAPTER FIVE

Putting on the Dog

Good grooming is necessary not only to keep your dog looking his best, but also for good health. A regular grooming routine will keep you in touch with your dog and enable you to detect anything out of the ordinary.

COAT CARE

The Australian Shepherd's wonderful coat helps make him a versatile working dog, able to function in just about any climate. This double coat, with silky outer guard hair and a thick, softer undercoat, is also easy to keep up. It does not mat (tangle into knots), nor does it need to be trimmed.

This coat does have a drawback, though. It sheds! Australian Shepherds shed heavily twice a year; normally in the spring and fall, although the exact time depends upon your climate and the dog's living conditions. However, the coat sheds a little all the time, all year-round. Regular coat care will help to reduce shedding on furniture and carpet.

Brushing

If you brush your Australian Shepherd thoroughly two to three times a week, you can keep the hair on the floor and carpet to a minimum. There are three grooming tools that you should use when brushing your Australian Shepherd.

First, use a pin brush to loosen clumps of coat, dirt, grass seeds, burrs or other debris. Use this brush first. Starting at the head, brush in the direction that the coat grows, from the head down to the tail.

Next, you will use a shedding blade to pull out the dead coat. With your dog still lying on his side, go over the dog from head to tail on each side.

Finish by going over the dog completely with a slicker brush. This will gather the loose hairs the other brushes left behind.

When you're done brushing your Australian Shepherd, you should have a dog with a clean shiny coat and a garbage bag (or vacuum bag) full of loose hair.

Bathing

Depending on your Australian Shepherd's living environment, you may wish to bathe him once a week or once a month. It doesn't matter how often you bathe your dog—even weekly won't hurt him—as long as you use a shampoo formulated for dogs that is gentle and conditioning.

When choosing a shampoo, ask your veterinarian or a dog groomer for his or her recommendations; there are so many shampoos on the market. When you buy the shampoo, read the instructions carefully. Put a cotton ball in each of your dog's ears to keep water out.

Once your Australian Shepherd is wet, put some shampoo on your hands and start working it into the

This owner uses a slicker brush to prepare the coat for final grooming.

42

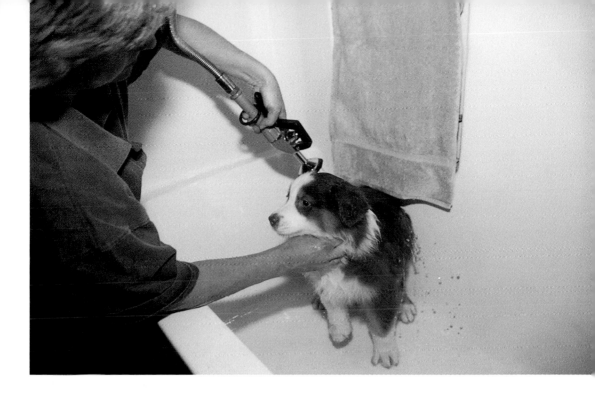

coat, starting at the head and ears and working down the neck. Be careful not to get soap in his eyes. Continue until the dog is covered with shampoo; don't forget his legs, tummy, groin and tail. Rinse thoroughly in the same manner, starting at his head and working down the body.

Once your Australian Shepherd is thoroughly rinsed, let him shake off the excess water. Now towel him dry and, if you wish, use your blow dryer to finish the job. Just be careful not to burn him with the dryer.

OTHER GROOMING PROCEDURES

Ear Cleaning

If the dog's ears are dirty or waxy, wet a cotton ball slightly with witch hazel and, using your finger, gently swab out the ear, getting the cotton ball into all the cracks and crevasses of the ear. You may want to use two or three cotton balls per ear. If the dog's ears have a sour smell or seem to be extremely dirty, or if the dog is pawing at his ears or shaking his head, call your veterinarian immediately.

Before his bath, make sure your Aussie is thoroughly brushed and then use the hose or shower to get him entirely wet.

or his eyes are red and irritated, call your veterinarian.

Dental Hygiene

If you start when your Australian Shepherd is a puppy, keeping your dog's teeth clean can be easy. Take some gauze from your first aid kit and wrap it around your index finger. Dampen it and dip it in baking soda. Take that baking soda and rub it over your dog's teeth, working gently over each tooth, the inside and the outside, and into the gum line, taking care not to hurt the dog. Do two or three teeth at a time, and let your dog have a drink. You may even want to break it into several sessions, doing half or a quarter of the dog's mouth at each session. Dental cleaning should be done at least three times a week.

Bathing your Aussie frequently won't hurt him as long as you use a shampoo that is formulated for dogs.

Eye Care

If your Australian Shepherd has some matter in the corners of his eyes, just use a damp paper towel to pick up the matter. However, if your dog has a different type of discharge,

QUICK AND PAINLESS NAIL CLIPPING

This is possible if you make a habit out of handling your dog's feet and giving your dog treats when you do. When it's time to clip nails, go through the same routine, but take your clippers and snip off just the ends of the nail—clip too far down and you'll cut into the "quick," the nerve center, hurting your dog and causing the nail to bleed. Clip two nails a session while you're getting your dog used to the procedure, and you'll soon be doing all four feet quickly and easily.

Nail Trimming

If your dog's nails get too long, they can actually deform the foot by applying pressure against the ground, causing the toes to bend in an unnatural position. Long nails are more prone to painful breaking and tearing.

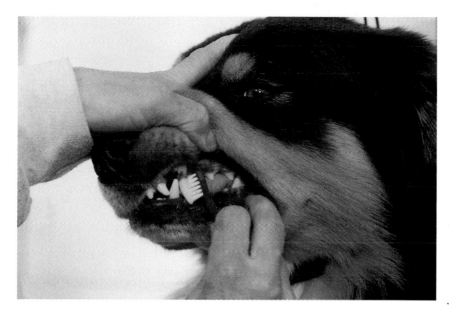

Brushing your Aussie's teeth often will keep his gums healthy and his breath fresh.

With your clippers in hand, have your dog lay down on the floor in front of you. Take one foot and pull the hair back from the nail so you can see the entire nail. If your dog's nails are black, you won't be able to see the quick, but if your Australian Shepherd has one or two white nails, you will be able to see the pink quick inside. If you cut into the quick when you are trimming the nails, the nail will bleed.

Take trimming very slowly. Look for a slight hook at the end of a long nail. You can safely trim that hook without hitting the quick. Then, very carefully, take just a little more.

If you hit the quick, take a bar of soap and rub the nail along the soap. The soap will clog the nail for a few minutes until the blood can clot. Now, while the soap is in the nail, hold that paw and look at the nail you cut. How far did you go? Trim the other nails, using that one as a guide but taking less off of the other nails.

If your Australian Shepherd dislikes nail trimming, try to make it as pleasant as possible. Have the nail clippers at hand. Have your dog lay down in front of you and then give him a massage, slowly and gently. When the dog is relaxed, touch one

Your dog's toenails need to be trimmed regularly.

of his feet, again, slowly and gently. Then go back to massaging. Then touch his feet again. By doing this, you are showing him that touching his feet is painless and is followed by more massaging.

When the dog will let you touch his paws without reacting, have the nail clippers in hand as you massage and then trim one nail. Just do one and then go back to massaging. When the dog is relaxed again, trim one more, and so on. If your dog is very frightened of nail trimming, you may want to break this down even further, doing one paw per massage session. Don't forget to reward your dog for allowing you to trim his nails by giving him his favorite treats. Your dog will begin to associate nail trimming with something pleasurable, allowing you to trim his nails with ease.

CHAPTER SIX

Measuring Up

WHAT IS A BREED STANDARD?

Each breed of dog recognized by a dog registry, such as the Australian Shepherd Club of America or the American Kennel Club (AKC), has a written description called the "standard." The standard is a verbal picture of the ideal dog of that breed, describing every aspect of her appearance and demeanor in detail. It is written by people with expert knowledge of the breed, usually a club or committee composed of long-time breeders, exhibitors and judges.

When a dog competes in a dog show, she is judged not only against the other dogs of her breed competing that day, but also against the written standard. The dog that wins is the dog that most closely fits the written description, compared to the other dogs competing. The standard is also used to choose dogs for breeding. Breeders use the standard as a guideline to determine which dogs or bitches should pass on their genes to future generations.

This Aussie demonstrates the breed's strength.

WHAT IS A BREED STANDARD?

A breed standard—a detailed description of an individual breed—is meant to portray the ideal specimen of that breed. This includes ideal structure, temperament, gait, type—all aspects of the dog. Because the standard describes an ideal specimen, it isn't based on any particular dog. It is a concept against which judges compare actual dogs and breeders strive to produce dogs. At a dog show, the dog that wins is the one that comes closest, in the judge's opinion, to the standard for its breed. Breed standards are written by the breed parent clubs, the national organizations formed to oversee the well-being of the breed. They are voted on and approved by the members of the parent clubs.

It is important to keep in mind when reading the standard and trying to match one's own Aussie to it that the standard describes an *ideal* Australian Shepherd, and some sections are geared toward a show interpretation.

What follow are descriptions of the ideal Australian Shepherd. Excerpts from the breed standard, as approved by the American Kennel Club (AKC) in 1993, appear in italics, and are followed by comments.

GENERAL APPEARANCE

The Australian Shepherd is an intelligent working dog with strong herding and guarding instincts. He is a loyal companion and has the stamina to work all day. He is well-balanced, slightly longer than tall and of medium size and bone, with color that offers variety and individuality. He is attentive and animated, lithe and agile, solid and muscular without cloddiness. He has a coat of moderate length and coarseness. He has a docked or natural bobbed tail.

This introductory paragraph sets the stage for the rest of the standard. It describes a well-proportioned dog of medium size capable of working hard—an athlete. Individuality is a trait of the breed; all Aussies are not meant to look the same, though they do have fundamental traits in common. This variety and large gene pool keep the breed vigorous and healthy.

he is good-natured and is seldom quarrelsome. He may be somewhat reserved in initial meetings. Faults: Any display of shyness, fear or aggression is to be severely penalized.

The dog should not be shy, fearful or aggressive toward people. An Australian Shepherd with the correct character or temperament is a dog willing to work for her owner, a dog to be treasured for her loyalty, intelligence and versatility.

Character and Temperament

The Australian Shepherd is an intelligent, active dog with an even disposition;

Head

The head is clean-cut, strong and dry. Overall size should be in proportion to the body. The muzzle is equal in length or slightly shorter than the back skull.

Her willingness to work for her owner is one of the breed's many fine qualities.

Aussies are loyal and eager to please those they love.

Viewed from the side, the topline of the back-skull and muzzle form parallel planes, divided by a moderate, well-defined stop. The muzzle tapers little from base to nose and is rounded at the tip.

Expression

Showing attentiveness and intelligence, alert and eager. Gaze should be keen but friendly.

Eyes

Eyes are brown, blue, amber or any variation or combination thereof, including flecks or marbling. Almond-shaped, not protruding nor sunken. The blue merles and blacks have black pigmentation on eye rims. The reds and red merles have liver (brown) pigmentation on eye rims.

Eye color in the Australian Shepherd is an outstanding feature of the breed. An individual Aussie may have different-colored eyes; a single iris may even have different colors in it.

Teeth

A full complement of strong, white teeth should meet in a scissors bite or may meet in a level bite. Disqualifications: Undershot, overshot by greater than 1/8 inch. Loss of contact caused by short center incisors in an otherwise correct bite shall not be judged undershot. Teeth missing or broken by accident shall not be penalized.

When the AKC standard was adopted, many people were concerned with the acceptance of a level or even bite. Most canine bite experts feel a scissors bite is indicative of a proper jaw assembly and the scissors bite allows a herding dog to properly "grip" livestock with a pinching motion instead of a puncturing bite. Other experts feel that teeth in an even jaw are more prone to wear by the constant meeting of teeth and are more apt to be injured or broken.

Ears

Ears are triangular of moderate size and leather, set high at the head. At full attention they break forward and over, or to the side as a rose ear. Prick ears and hanging ears are severe faults.

Neck and Body

Neck is strong, of moderate length slightly arched at the crest, fitting well into the shoulders.

Topline. Back is straight and strong, level and firm from withers to hip joints. The croup is moderately sloped.

Chest is not broad but is deep with the lowest point reaching the elbow. The

THE AMERICAN KENNEL CLUB

Familiarly referred to as "the AKC," the American Kennel Club is a nonprofit organization devoted to the advancement of purebred dogs. The AKC maintains a registry of recognized breeds and adopts and enforces rules for dog events including shows, obedience trials, field trials, hunting tests, lure coursing, herding, earthdog trials, agility and the Canine Good Citizen program. It is a club of clubs, established in 1884 and composed, today, of over 500 autonomous dog clubs throughout the United States. Each club is represented by a delegate; the delegates make up the legislative body of the AKC, voting on rules and electing directors. The American Kennel Club maintains the Stud Book, the record of every dog ever registered with the AKC, and publishes a variety of materials on purebred dogs, including a monthly magazine, books and numerous educational pamphlets. For more information, contact the AKC at the address listed in Chapter 9, "Resources."

ribs are well-sprung and long, neither barrel chested nor slab sided. The underline shows a moderate tuck-up.

Tail is straight, docked or naturally bobbed, not to exceed four inches in length.

The neck and body section describes a fit, strong dog that is versatile and able to work hard and efficiently.

This Australian Shepherd's coat color is blue merle—blue blotches against a lighter background of the same pigment.

Color

Blue merle, black, red merle, red—all with or without white marking and/or tan (copper) points, with no order of preference. The hairline of a white collar does not exceed the point of the withers at the skin. White is acceptable on the neck (either in part or as a full collar) chest, legs, muzzle, underparts, blaze on head and white extension up to four inches measuring from a horizontal line at the elbow. White on the head should not predominate and the eyes must be fully surrounded by color and pigment. Merles characteristically become darker with increasing age. Disqualifications: White body splashes.

This Aussie sports a black coat.

A red merle (left) and a red-coated Aussie (right).

Gait

The Australian Shepherd has a smooth, free and easy gait. He exhibits great agility of movement with a well-balanced, ground covering stride. Fore and hind legs move straight and parallel with the center line of the body. As speed increases, the feet, front and rear, converge towards the center line of gravity of the dog while the back remains firm and level. The Australian Shepherd must be agile and able to change direction or gait instantly.

The breed's heritage as an active herding dog required this. Today, as a breed active in many dog sports, including obedience, agility and flyball, a natural athleticism is needed.

Size

The preferred height for males is 20–23 inches and females 18–21 inches. Quality is not to be sacrificed in favor of size.

Proportion

Measuring from breastbone to the rear of the thigh and from the top of the withers to the ground, the Australian Shepherd is slightly longer than tall.

Substance

Solidly built with moderate bone. Structure in males reflects masculinity *without coarseness. Bitches appear feminine without being slight of bone.*

UNDERSTANDING WHAT THE WORDS MEAN

If you're having trouble picturing in your mind what these words actually mean, try reading the standard with your Australian Shepherd standing in front of you. Compare the words to your dog. Do you see what they are describing?

If you still have questions, go to a dog show and find people with Australian Shepherds. Ask a couple of different people how they interpret the standard, or portions of the standard, and ask them to demonstrate on a dog. Also, after the judging is completed, many judges will be happy to express an opinion about the standard and dogs in general.

Australian Shepherd clubs often host seminars, where judges and breeders speak on a variety of subjects, including the breed standard. Ask your local club if anything is planned for the future.

The different viewpoints expressed by a variety of people will either clarify the standard for you or totally confuse you. Just keep in mind that the standard is made up of words, and words have different

In addition to being great athletes, Australian Shepherds are fun-loving and playful.

meanings to different people, so there will always be some differences in opinion. Also, applying the descriptions, no matter how well they are written, to living, breathing dogs can be very difficult.

The Australian Shepherd has an alert, intelligent expression. Your Australian Shepherd will probably not fit all the requirements of the standard, but she will still be a loyal friend and companion. Aussies' eyes are an outstanding feature of the breed, and can be multi-colored, marbled or flecked. The Aussie's herding heritage has produced a strong, athletic working dog.

The Australian Shepherd is, first and foremost, an athlete.

55

CHAPTER SEVEN

A Matter of Fact

HERDING HERITAGE

The first occupation for dogs was guarding the family or tribe's cave, warning of predators and trespassers. Dogs most certainly helped on the hunt for food, and as mankind domesticated other animals, dogs were used to protect and care for the family's livestock. As humans began to depend more and more on livestock and less on hunting, protection of herds became necessary to ensure a family's livelihood and sustenance.

Herding dogs became critical to mankind's survival.

Herding dogs were bred to work in numerous terrains and climates with a variety of livestock, including sheep, goats, cattle and ducks. Over thousands of years, herding dogs of various types were developed all over the world.

It is from this mix of herding breeds that the Australian Shepherd most likely evolved, but the breed's early history is unknown. Some breed historians feel that the Aussie is a mixture of herding breeds that came to America with early settlers from Europe. Other researchers are convinced that the breed originated in Europe, went to Australia and then came to California and North America during the Gold Rush. Below, we'll briefly explore the possible origins of the Aussie.

HERDING DOGS IN THE NEW WORLD

Early American history is threaded with bits of information concerning sheep, shepherds and their herding dogs. Christopher Columbus, who made four trips to the New World (1492–1502), brought sheep with him to North America on at least two of his trips.

The British explorers (early 1600's) did not bring sheep with them that we know of, but the settlers who followed them did, and with these sheep came their dogs.

The Spanish also figured prominently among settlers who brought domestic animals to the New World. Merino sheep and their wonderful wool had ensured Spain a primary place in the world trade markets in the 1500s and 1600s, and sheep were the mainstay of the economy. When Spanish immigrants came to the Americas, both North and South, they brought their sheep.

By the late 1600s and early 1700s, immigrants from several nations were flooding into North

Australian Shepherds are considered herding dogs.

An Aussie doing what he was bred to do.

America, bringing their livestock and dogs with them to the New World. Immigrants from Scotland brought the Scottish Collie (a Bearded Collie-type dog) with them; immigrants from Wales brought along the Welsh Grey Sheepdog, also a Bearded Collie-type dog. The French imported the Bouvier des Flandres and the Germans, who also brought Merino sheep to the New World, brought along their German Shepherds and the Hutespitz, a Spitz-type dog.

One of the popular herding dogs imported was the English Shepherd. Called a "farm collie" or "ranch collie" in early America, the English Shepherd could herd livestock, protect the family against wild animals and warn off trespassers. The English Shepherd today looks much like an Australian Shepherd with a tail. This similarity suggests to many that the English Shepherd is an ancestor of today's Australian Shepherd, though there is no definitive way to prove it.

As immigrants and their dogs settled in America from all over Europe, crossings of the various breeds took place. Eventually, as the different regions were settled and communities were established, each area developed a particular type of herding dog suited to its particular needs.

THE AUSTRALIAN SHEPHERD IN THE AMERICAN WEST

The California Gold Rush brought a flood of people to California. Some sought to make their fortunes panning for gold, while others made a fortune selling equipment to the miners, often at outrageous prices. Food was sometimes in short supply, and flocks of sheep were brought in to feed and clothe the hordes.

A loyal, trainable herding dog was needed and the Aussie, as the breed type was beginning to be known, fit right in. Stories abound as to how the breed became known as the "Australian Shepherd." Photographs, notes in personal diaries, stories told to grandchildren and old photographs show us that a dog very similar to today's Aussie was an integral part of early North American, and especially Western, life.

But where did he come from? He might be a cross-breeding of British-type herding dogs that served as farm dogs all over the country or he might have come from the Basque country of Europe by way of Australia. Or

WHERE DID DOGS COME FROM?

It can be argued that dogs were right there at man's side from the beginning of time. As soon as human beings began to document their existence, the dog was among their drawings and inscriptions. Dogs were not just friends, they served a purpose: There were dogs to hunt birds, pull sleds, herd sheep, burrow after rats— even sit in laps! What your dog was originally bred to do influences the way he behaves. The American Kennel Club recognizes over 140 breeds, and there are hundreds more distinct breeds around the world. To make sense of the breeds, they are grouped according to their size or function. The AKC has seven groups:

1. Sporting
2. Working
3. Herding
4. Hounds
5. Terriers
6. Toys
7. Non Sporting

Can you name a breed from each group? Here's some help: (1) Golden Retriever; (2) Doberman Pinscher; (3) Collie; (4) Beagle; (5) Scottish Terrier; (6) Maltese; and (7) Dalmatian. All modern domestic dogs (*Canis familiaris*) are related, however different they look, and are all descended from *Canis lupus,* the gray wolf.

This mother and pup don't know why they are called Australian Shepherds; they are very much an American breed.

he might be a combination of all of the above. Like many Americans, the Aussie is very much a part of the American melting pot.

THE AUSSIE IN AUSTRALIA

In the 1700s, people were immigrating to Australia as well as to North America. The Germans, French, Irish, Welsh and English moved there, bringing their livestock and dogs. The German Coulie is a herding dog that looks much like today's Aussie and might figure in the breed's heritage. The British immigrated in large numbers, infusing Australia

with their customs, language and, of course, their dogs.

As the popularity of sheep herding spread throughout Australia, herding dogs became a necessity. When Merino sheep were imported, Spanish and Basque shepherds came to care for them, bringing their Pyrenees sheepdogs and Catalan sheepdogs. As in North America, a lot of mixed breeding took place, some intentional, some by accident.

THE BASQUE FACTOR

The Basque people live in the western Pyrenees in France and Spain. They are credited with the development of some wonderful herding dogs, including, some say, the ancestors of the Australian Shepherd. Many Aussie historians believe that the modern Aussie is the descendant of Basque sheepdogs that went to Australia and then to North America, following the herds of sheep.

THE AUSSIE BECOMES ESTABLISHED

Over the years, a breed type began to emerge. People appreciated the intelligence, trainability and athleticism of the Aussies, and they tried to breed similar dogs together to retain these treasured traits. In the western United States, some dedicated fans of the breed began to popularize the Aussie by spreading the word about this talented breed.

THE AUSSIE TODAY

The versatility of the Australian Shepherd is remarkable. Today's Australian Shepherd is an active and intelligent companion that requires stimulation and activity. The breed's easy trainability, intelligence, common sense and problem-solving abilities, combined with a medium-size build, an

easy-to-care-for coat, a strong will to work and incredible loyalty make for a great working and playing companion.

In 1991, the Australian Shepherd was admitted into the American Kennel Club. Some feared this would mean the breed's deterioration into an attractive show dog with little working ability. After several attempts, however, admission into the AKC was final. The Australian Shepherd can now participate in any activity sponsored by the AKC, including obedience, agility and tracking competitions.

Stockdog

As we have seen, the breed's first occupation was as a stockdog. Aussies are able to work a variety of livestock in different situations and terrain. They can be soft enough to work ewes and lambs and tough enough

61

Intelligence, trainability, athleticism and loyalty are the Aussie's most relished attributes.

to handle range cattle. Aussies can drive, move and gather livestock on the range, in a small farm setting or in stockdog trials.

Search and Rescue

The Aussie's strong work ethic, intelligence and good scenting abilities have made him a premier search and rescue dog. Trained dogs and their owners have found lost hikers, children who have wandered away and elderly people who have become confused and lost. Search and rescue–trained Aussies have worked to find flood victims and people swept away by mudslides and avalanches.

Tracking

Tracking is an activity that allows the Australian Shepherd to use his naturally acute sense of smell. Tracking can be a competitive sport in which prizes and titles are awarded, it can

There's nothing more rewarding than spending time with a happy dog.

be a recreational activity ("Go find Dad! Where is he?") or it can be part of a search and rescue effort.

Service Dogs

Service dogs work to provide personal assistance to their physically challenged owners. These dogs might retrieve dropped items, open doors, get items out of the refrigerator or pull wheelchairs. Hearing-alert dogs notify their owner of noises in the environment, including smoke detectors and a baby's crying. Service dogs provide their owners with aid, independence and an important social icebreaker. After all, everyone wants to talk about a working dog.

Guide Dogs

Most guide dogs are larger breeds, such as German Shepherd Dogs or Labrador Retrievers. However, a larger dog can also cause larger problems. Several guide dog schools started using the Australian Shepherd several years ago and have found the breed to be very good at this work. When partnered with teenagers, women or smaller men, the breed has been up to the challenge, and, in fact, worked

out better than anyone (except of course, an Aussie fan!) expected.

Therapy Dogs

Therapy dogs go with their owners to nursing homes, schools, day care centers and hospitals and share love and affection with people who need it. Many people assume that because Aussies are supposed to be reserved with strangers and protective of their people, the breed cannot work as a therapy dog, but nothing is further from the truth. If an Australian Shepherd is well socialized to many different people as a puppy and young dog, he will quickly learn what is expected during therapy dog work.

Aussies play flyball, excel in agility, pull wagons, go hiking—even leap tall logs in a single bound.

CHAPTER EIGHT

On Good Behavior

by Ian Dunbar, Ph.D., MRCVS

Training is the jewel in the crown—the most important aspect of doggy husbandry. There is no more important variable influencing dog behavior and temperament than the dog's education: A well-trained, well-behaved and good-natured puppydog is always a joy to live with, but an untrained and uncivilized dog can be a perpetual nightmare. Moreover, deny the dog an education and she will not have the opportunity to fulfill her own canine potential; neither will she have the ability to communicate effectively with her human companions.

Luckily, modern psychological training methods are easy, efficient, effective and, above all, considerably dog-friendly and user-friendly. Doggy education is as simple as it is enjoyable. But before you can have a good time play-training with your new dog, you have to learn what to do and how to do it. There is no big-ger variable influencing the success of dog training than the owner's ex-perience and expertise. Before you embark on the dog's education, you must first educate yourself.

BASIC TRAINING FOR OWNERS

Ideally, basic owner training should begin well before you select your dog. Find out all you can about your chosen breed first, then master rudimentary training and handl-ing skills. If you already have your puppydog, owner training is a dire emergency—the clock is ticking! Especially for puppies, the first few weeks at home are the most impor-tant and influential days in the dog's life. Indeed, the cause of most ado-lescent and adult problems may be traced back to the initial days the pup explores her new home. This is the time to establish the *status quo*—to teach the puppydog how you would like her to behave and so

This owner and her Aussie enjoy a training session.

OWNING A PARTY ANIMAL

It's a fact: The more of the world your puppy is exposed to, the more comfortable she'll be in it. Once your puppy's had her shots, start taking her everywhere with you. Encourage friendly interaction with strangers, expose her to different environments (towns, fields, beaches) and most important, enroll her in a puppy class where she'll get to play with other puppies. These simple, fun, shared activities will develop your pup into a confident socialite; reliable around other people and dogs.

prevent otherwise quite predictable problems.

In addition to consulting breeders and breed books such as this one (which understandably have a positive breed bias), seek out as many pet owners with your breed as you can find. Good points are obvious. What you want to find out are the breed-specific problems, so you can nip them in the bud. In particular, you should talk to owners with adolescent dogs and make a list of all anticipated problems. Most important, test drive at least half a dozen adolescent and adult dogs of your breed yourself. An 8-week-old puppy is deceptively easy to handle, but she will acquire adult size, speed and strength in just four months, so you should learn now what to prepare for.

Puppy and pet dog training classes offer a convenient venue to locate pet owners and observe dogs in action. For a list of suitable trainers in your area, contact the Association of Pet Dog Trainers (see chapter 9). You may also begin your basic owner training by observing other owners in class. Watch as many classes and test drive as many dogs as possible. Select an upbeat, dog-friendly, people-friendly, fun-and-games, puppydog pet training class to learn the ropes. Also, watch training videos and read training books. You must find out what to do and how to do it *before* you have to do it.

PRINCIPLES OF TRAINING

Most people think training comprises teaching the dog to do things such as sit, speak and roll over, but even a 4-week-old pup knows how to do these things already. Instead, the first step in training involves teaching the dog human words for each dog behavior and activity and for each aspect of the dog's environment.

That way you, the owner, can more easily participate in the dog's domestic education by directing her to perform specific actions appropriately, that is, at the right time, in the right place and so on. Training opens communication channels, enabling an educated dog to at least understand her owner's requests.

In addition to teaching a dog what we want her to do, it is also necessary to teach her why she should do what we ask. Indeed, 95 percent of training revolves around motivating the dog to want to do what we want. Dogs often understand what their owners want; they just don't see the point of doing it—especially when the owner's repetitively boring and seemingly senseless instructions are totally at odds with much more pressing and exciting doggy distractions. It is not so much the dog that is being stubborn or dominant; rather, it is the owner who has failed to acknowledge the dog's needs and feelings and to approach training from the dog's point of view.

The Meaning of Instructions

The secret to successful training is learning how to use training lures to predict or prompt specific behaviors—to coax the dog to do what you want when you want. Any highly valued object (such as a treat or toy) may be used as a lure, which the dog will follow with her eyes and nose. Moving the lure in specific ways entices the dog to move her nose, head and entire body in specific ways. In fact, by learning the art of manipulating various lures, it is possible to teach the dog to assume virtually any body position and perform any action. Once you have control over the expression of the dog's behaviors and can elicit any body position or

There are many different lures you can use to train your dog. Try some liver, your dog's favorite treat, a stuffed chew toy or her favorite stuffed animal.

FINDING A TRAINER

Have fun with your dog, take a training class! But don't just sign on any dotted line, find a trainer whose approach and style you like and whose students (and their dogs) are really learning. Ask to visit a class to observe a trainer in action. For the names of trainers near you, ask your veterinarian, your pet supply store, your dog-owning neighbors or call (800) PET-DOGS (the Association of Pet Dog Trainers.)

behavior at will, you can easily teach the dog to perform on request.

Tell your dog what you want her to do, use a lure to entice her to respond correctly, then profusely praise and maybe reward her once she performs the desired action. For example, verbally request "Fido, sit!" while you move a squeaky toy upwards and backwards over the dog's muzzle (lure-movement and hand signal), smile knowingly as she looks up (to follow the lure) and sits down (as a result of canine anatomical engineering), then praise her to distraction ("Gooood Fido!"). Squeak the toy, offer a training treat and give your dog and yourself a pat on the back.

Being able to elicit desired responses over and over enables the owner to reward the dog over and over. Consequently, the dog begins to think training is fun. For example, the more the dog is rewarded for sitting, the more she enjoys sitting. Eventually the dog comes to realize that, whereas most sitting is appreciated, sitting immediately upon request usually prompts especially enthusiastic praise and a slew of high-level rewards. The dog begins to sit on cue much of the time, showing that she is starting to grasp the meaning of the owner's verbal request and hand signal.

Why Comply?

Most dogs enjoy initial lure-reward training and are only too happy to comply with their owners' wishes. Unfortunately, repetitive drilling without appreciative feedback tends to diminish the dog's enthusiasm until she eventually fails to see the point of complying anymore. Moreover, as the dog approaches adolescence she becomes more easily distracted as she develops other interests. Lengthy sessions with repetitive exercises tend to bore and demotivate both parties. If it's not fun, the owner doesn't do it and neither does the dog.

Integrate training into your dog's life: The greater number of training sessions each day and the shorter they are, the more willingly compliant your dog will become. Make sure to have a short (just a few seconds) training interlude before every enjoyable canine activity. For example, ask your dog to sit to greet people, to sit before you throw her Frisbee and to sit for her supper. Really, sitting is no different from a canine "Please." Also, include numerous short training interludes during every enjoyable canine pastime, for example, when playing with the dog or when she is running in the park. In this fashion, doggy distractions may be effectively converted into rewards for training. Just as all games have rules, fun becomes training . . . and training becomes fun.

Eventually, rewards actually become unnecessary to continue motivating your dog. If trained with consideration and kindness, performing the desired behaviors will become self rewarding and, in a sense, your dog will motivate herself. Just as it is not necessary to reward a human companion during an enjoyable walk in the park, or following a game of tennis, it is hardly necessary to reward our best friend—the dog—for walking by our side or while playing fetch. Human company during enjoyable

activities is reward enough for most dogs.

Even though your dog has become self-motivating, it's still good to praise and pet her a lot and offer rewards once in a while, especially for a good job well done. And if for no other reason, praising and rewarding others is good for the human heart.

TRAINER'S TOOLS

Many training books extol the virtues of a vast array of training paraphernalia and electronic and metallic gizmos, most of which are designed for canine restraint, correction and punishment, rather than for actual facilitation of

69

As your Aussie reaches adolescence, explore new, fun ways to keep her interested in training.

Taking your Aussie on an enjoyable walk is one great way to reward her for being on good behavior.

doggy education. In reality, most effective training tools are not found in stores; they come from within ourselves.

In terms of equipment, all dogs do require a quality buckle collar to sport dog tags and to attach the leash (for safety and to comply with local leash laws). Hollow chew toys (like Kongs or sterilized longbones) and a dog bed or collapsible crate are musts for housetraining. Three additional tools are required:

1. specific lures (training treats and toys) to predict and prompt specific desired behaviors;

2. rewards (praise, affection, training treats and toys) to reinforce for the dog what a lot of fun it all is; and

3. knowledge—how to convert the dog's favorite activities and games (potential distractions to training) into "life-rewards," which may be employed to facilitate training.

The most powerful of these is knowledge. Education is the key! Watch training classes, participate in training classes, watch videos, read books, enjoy play-training with your dog and then your dog will say "Please," and your dog will say "Thank you!"

HOUSETRAINING

If dogs were left to their own devices, certainly they would chew, dig and bark for entertainment and then no doubt highlight a few areas of their living space with sprinkles of urine, in much the same way we decorate by hanging pictures. Consequently, when we ask a dog to live with us, we must teach her *where* she may dig, *where* she may perform her toilet duties, *what* she may chew and *when* she may bark. After all, when left at home alone for many hours, we cannot expect the dog to amuse herself by completing crosswords or watching the soaps on TV!

Also, it would be decidedly unfair to keep the house rules a secret from the dog, and then get angry and punish the poor critter for inevitably transgressing rules she did not even know existed. Remember: Without adequate education and guidance, the dog will be forced to establish her own rules—doggy rules—and most probably will be at odds with the owner's view of domestic living.

Since most problems develop during the first few days the dog is at home, prospective dog owners must

HOUSETRAINING 1-2-3

1. Prevent Mistakes. When you can't supervise your puppy, confine her in a single room or in her crate (but don't leave her for too long!). Puppy-proof the area by laying down newspapers so that if she does make a mistake, it won't matter.

2. Teach Where. Take your puppy to the spot you want her to use every hour.

3. When she goes, praise her profusely and give her three favorite treats.

71

In addition to a willing dog, the only tools you really need to train are common sense, gentle hands, a loving heart and a good attitude.

be certain they are quite clear about the principles of housetraining *before* they get a dog. Early misbehaviors quickly become established as the *status quo*—becoming firmly entrenched as hard-to-break bad habits, which set the precedent for years to come. Make sure to teach your dog good habits right from the start. Good habits are just as hard to break as bad ones!

Ideally, when a new dog comes home, try to arrange for someone to be present as much as possible during the first few days (for adult dogs) or weeks for puppies. With only a little forethought, it is surprisingly easy to find a puppy sitter, such as a retired person, who would be willing to eat from your refrigerator and watch your television while keeping an eye on the newcomer to encourage the dog to play with chew toys and to ensure she goes outside on a regular basis.

Potty Training

To teach the dog where to relieve herself:

1. never let her make a single mistake;

2. let her know where you want her to go; and

3. handsomely reward her for doing so: "GOOOOOOOD DOG!!!" liver treat, liver treat, liver treat!

Preventing Mistakes

A single mistake is a training disaster, since it heralds many more in future weeks. And each time the dog soils the house, this further reinforces the dog's unfortunate preference for an indoor, carpeted toilet. Do not let an unhousetrained dog have full run of the house.

When you are away from home, or cannot pay full attention, confine the dog to an area where elimination is appropriate, such as an outdoor run or, better still, a small, comfortable indoor kennel with access to an outdoor run. When confined in this manner, most dogs will naturally housetrain themselves.

If that's not possible, confine the dog to an area, such as a utility room, kitchen, basement or garage, where elimination may not be desired in the long run but as an interim measure it is certainly preferable to doing it all around the house. Use newspaper to cover the floor of the dog's day room. The newspaper may be used to soak up the urine and to wrap up and dispose of the feces. Once your dog develops a preferred spot for eliminating, it is only necessary to cover that part of the floor with newspaper. The smaller papered area may then be moved (only a little each day) towards the door to the outside. Thus the dog will develop the tendency to go to the door when she needs to relieve herself.

Never confine an unhousetrained dog to a crate for long periods. Doing so would force the dog to soil the crate and ruin its usefulness as an aid for housetraining (see the following discussion).

Teaching Where

In order to teach your dog where you would like her to do her business, you have to be there to direct the proceedings—an obvious, yet often neglected, fact of life. In order to be there to teach the dog where to go, you need to know *when* she needs to go. Indeed, the success of housetraining depends on the owner's ability to predict these times. Certainly, a regular feeding schedule will facilitate prediction somewhat, but there is nothing like "loading the deck" and influencing the timing of the outcome yourself!

Whenever you are at home, make sure the dog is under constant supervision and/or confined to a small area. If already well trained, simply instruct the dog to lie down in her bed or basket. Alternatively, confine the dog to a crate (doggy den) or tie-down (a short, 18-inch lead that can be clipped to an eye hook in the baseboard near her bed). Short-term close confinement strongly inhibits urination and defecation, since the dog does not want to soil her sleeping area. Thus, when you release the puppydog each hour, she will definitely need to urinate immediately and defecate every third or fourth hour. Keep the dog confined

73

A well-house-trained dog often asks when it's time to go out.

Short-term, close confinement strongly inhibits urination and defecation.

74

to her doggy den and take her to her intended toilet area each hour, every hour and on the hour. When taking your dog outside, instruct her to sit quietly before opening the door— she will soon learn to sit by the door when she needs to go out!

Teaching Why

Being able to predict when the dog needs to go enables the owner to be on the spot to praise and reward the dog. Each hour, hurry the dog to the intended toilet area in the yard, issue the appropriate instruction ("Go pee!" or "Go poop!"), then give the dog three to four minutes to produce. Praise and offer a couple of training treats when successful. The treats are important because many people fail to praise their dogs with feeling . . . and housetraining is hardly the time for understatement. So either loosen up and enthusiastically praise that dog: "Wuzzzer-wuzzer-wuzzer, hoooser good wuffer den? Hoooo went pee for Daddy?" Or say "Good dog!" as best you can and offer the treats for effect.

Following elimination is an ideal time for a spot of play-training in the yard or house. Also, an empty dog may be allowed greater freedom around the house for the next half hour or so, just as long as you keep an eye out to make sure she does not get into other kinds of mischief. If you are preoccupied and cannot pay full attention, confine the dog to her doggy den once more to enjoy a peaceful snooze or to play with her many chew toys.

If your dog does not eliminate within the allotted time outside—no biggie! Back to her doggy den, and then try again after another hour.

As I own large dogs, I always feel more relaxed walking an empty dog, knowing that I will not need to finish our stroll weighted down with bags of feces!

Beware of falling into the trap of walking the dog to get her to eliminate. The good ol' dog walk is such an enormous highlight in the dog's life that it represents the single biggest potential reward in domestic dogdom. However, when in a hurry, or during inclement weather, many owners abruptly terminate the walk the moment the dog has done her business. This, in effect, severely punishes the dog for doing the right thing, in the right place at the right time. Consequently, many dogs become strongly inhibited from eliminating outdoors because they know it will signal an abrupt end to an otherwise thoroughly enjoyable walk.

Instead, instruct the dog to relieve herself in the yard prior to going for a walk. If you follow the above instructions, most dogs soon learn to eliminate on cue. As soon as the dog eliminates, praise (and offer a treat or two)—"Good dog! Let's go walkies!" Use the walk as a reward for eliminating in the yard. If the dog does not go, put her back in her doggy den and think about a walk later on. You will find with a "No feces—no walk" policy, your dog will

become one of the fastest defecators in the business.

If you do not have a backyard, instruct the dog to eliminate right outside your front door prior to the walk. Not only will this facilitate clean up and disposal of the feces in your own trash can but, also, the walk may again be used as a colossal reward.

CHEWING AND BARKING

Short-term close confinement also teaches the dog that occasional quiet moments are a reality of domestic living. Your puppydog is extremely impressionable during her first few weeks at home. Regular confinement at this time soon exerts a calming influence over the dog's personality. Remember, once the dog is housetrained and calmer, there will be a whole lifetime ahead for the dog to enjoy full run of the house and garden. On the other hand, by letting the newcomer have unrestricted access to the entire household and allowing her to run willy-nilly, she will most certainly develop a bunch of behavior problems in short order, no doubt necessitating confinement later in life. It would not be fair to remedially restrain and confine a dog

TOYS THAT EARN THEIR KEEP

To entertain even the most distracted of dogs, while you're home or away, have a selection of the following toys on hand: hollow chew toys (like Kongs, sterilized hollow longbones and cubes or balls that can be stuffed with kibble). Smear peanut butter or honey on the inside of the hollow toy or bone and stuff the bone with kibble and your dog will think of nothing else but working the object to get at the food. Great to take your dog's mind off the fact that you've left the house.

you have trained, through neglect, to run free.

When confining the dog, make sure she always has an impressive array of suitable chew toys. Kongs and sterilized longbones (both readily available from pet stores) make the best chew toys, since they are hollow and may be stuffed with treats to heighten the dog's interest. For example, by stuffing the little hole at the top of a Kong with a small piece of freeze-dried liver, the dog will not want to leave it alone.

Remember, treats do not have to be junk food and they certainly should not represent extra calories. Rather, treats should be part of each dog's regular daily diet: Some food may be served in the dog's bowl for breakfast and dinner, some food may be used as training treats, and some food may be used for stuffing chew toys. I regularly stuff my dogs' many Kongs with different shaped biscuits and kibble. The kibble seems to fall out fairly easily, as do the oval-shaped biscuits, thus rewarding the dog instantaneously for checking out the chew toys. The bone-shaped biscuits fall out after a while, rewarding the dog for worrying at the chew toy. But the triangular biscuits never come out. They remain inside the Kong as lures, maintaining the dog's fascination with her chew toy. To further focus the dog's interest, I always make sure to flavor the triangular biscuits by rubbing them with a little cheese or freeze-dried liver.

If stuffed chew toys are reserved especially for times the dog is confined, the puppydog will soon learn to enjoy quiet moments in her doggy den and she will quickly develop a chew-toy habit—a good habit! This is a simple autoshaping process; all the owner has to do is set up the situation and the dog all but trains herself—easy and effective. Even when the dog is given run of the house, her first inclination will be to indulge her rewarding chew-toy habit rather than destroy less-attractive household articles, such as curtains, carpets, chairs and compact disks. Similarly, a chew-toy chewer will be less inclined to scratch and chew herself excessively. Also, if the dog busies herself as a recreational chewer, she will be less inclined to develop into a recreational barker or digger when left at home alone.

Stuff a number of chew toys whenever the dog is left confined and remove the extra-special-tasting treats when you return. Your dog will now amuse herself with her chew toys before falling asleep and then resume playing with her chew toys when she expects you to return. Since most owner-absent misbehavior happens right after you leave and

right before your expected return, your puppydog will now be conveniently preoccupied with her chew toys at these times.

COME AND SIT

Most puppies will happily approach virtually anyone, whether called or not; that is, until they collide with adolescence and develop other more important doggy interests, such as sniffing a multiplicity of exquisite odors on the grass. Your mission, Mr./Ms. Owner, is to teach and reward the pup for coming reliably, willingly and happily when called—and you have just three months to get it done. Unless adequately reinforced, your puppy's tendency to approach people will self-destruct by adolescence.

77

To teach come, call your dog, open your arms as a welcoming signal, wave a toy or a treat and praise for every step in your direction.

Call your dog ("Fido, come!"), open your arms (and maybe squat down) as a welcoming signal, waggle a treat or toy as a lure and reward the puppydog when she comes running. Do not wait to praise the dog until she reaches you—she may come 95 percent of the way and then run off after some distraction. Instead, praise the dog's first step towards you and continue praising enthusiastically for every step she takes in your direction.

When the rapidly approaching puppy dog is three lengths away from impact, instruct her to sit ("Fido, sit!") and hold the lure in front of you in an outstretched hand to prevent her from hitting you mid-chest and knocking you flat on your back! As Fido decelerates to nose the lure, move the treat upwards and backwards just over her muzzle with an upwards motion of your extended arm (palm-upwards). As the dog looks up to follow the lure, she will sit down (if she jumps up, you are holding the lure too high). Praise the dog for sitting. Move backwards and call her again. Repeat this many times over, always praising when Fido comes and sits; on occasion, reward her.

For the first couple of trials, use a training treat both as a lure to entice the dog to come and sit and as a reward for doing so. Thereafter, try to use different items as lures and rewards. For example, lure the dog with a Kong or Frisbee but reward her with a food treat. Or lure the dog with a food treat but pat her and throw a tennis ball as a reward. After just a few repetitions, dispense with the lures and rewards; the dog will begin to respond willingly to your verbal requests and hand signals just for the prospect of praise from your heart and affection from your hands.

Instruct every family member, friend and visitor how to get the dog to come and sit. Invite people over for a series of pooch parties; do not keep the pup a secret—let other people enjoy this puppy, and let the pup enjoy other people. Puppydog parties are not only fun, they easily attract a lot of people to help you train your dog. Unless you teach your dog how to meet people, that is, to sit for greetings, no doubt the dog will resort to jumping up. Then you and the visitors will get annoyed, and the dog will be punished. This is not fair. Send out those invitations for puppy parties and teach your dog to be mannerly and socially acceptable.

Even though your dog quickly masters obedient recalls in the house, her reliability may falter when playing in the backyard or local park. Ironically, it is the owner who has unintentionally trained the dog not to respond in these instances. By allowing the dog to play and run around and otherwise have a good time, but then to call the dog to put her on leash to take her home, the dog quickly learns playing is fun but training is a drag. Thus, playing in the park becomes a severe distraction, which works against training. Bad news!

Instead, whether playing with the dog off leash or on leash, request her to come at frequent intervals—say, every minute or so. On most occasions, praise and pet the dog for a few seconds while she is sitting, then tell her to go play again. For especially fast recalls, offer a couple of training treats and take the time to praise and pet the dog enthusiastically before releasing her. The dog will learn that coming when called is not necessarily the end of the play session, and neither is it the end of the world; rather, it signals an enjoyable, quality timeout with the owner before resuming play once more. In fact, playing in the park now becomes a very effective life-reward, which works to facilitate training by reinforcing each obedient and timely recall. Good news!

SIT, DOWN, STAND AND ROLLOVER

Teaching the dog a variety of body positions is easy for owner and dog, impressive for spectators and extremely useful for all. Using lure-reward techniques, it is possible to train several positions at once to verbal commands or hand signals (which impress the socks off onlookers).

Sit and down—the two control commands—prevent or resolve nearly a hundred behavior problems. For example, if the dog happily and obediently sits or lies down when requested, she cannot jump on visitors, dash out the front door, run around and chase her tail, pester other dogs, harass cats or annoy family, friends or strangers. Additionally, "Sit" or "Down" are the best emergency commands for off-leash control.

It is easier to teach and maintain a reliable sit than maintain a reliable recall. Sit is the purest and simplest of commands—either the dog is sitting or she is not. If there is any change of circumstances or potential danger in the park, for example, simply instruct the dog to sit. If she sits, you have a number of options: Allow the dog to resume playing when she is safe, walk up and put the dog on leash or call the dog. The dog will be much more likely to come when called if she has already acknowledged her compliance by sitting. If the dog does not sit in the park—train her to!

Stand and rollover-stay are the two positions for examining the dog. Your veterinarian will love you to distraction if you take a little time to teach the dog to stand still and roll over and play possum. Also, your vet bills will be smaller because it will take the veterinarian less time to examine your dog. The rollover-stay is an especially useful command and is really just a variation of the down-stay: Whereas the dog lies prone in the traditional down, she lies supine in the rollover-stay.

As with teaching come and sit, the training techniques to teach the dog to assume all other body positions on cue are user-friendly and dog-friendly. Simply give the appropriate request, lure the dog into the desired body position using a training treat or toy and then praise (and maybe reward) the dog as soon as she complies. Try not to touch the dog to get her to respond. If you teach the dog by guiding her into position, the dog will quickly learn that rump-pressure means sit, for example, but as yet you

still have no control over your dog if she is just 6 feet away. It will still be necessary to teach the dog to sit on request. So do not make training a time-consuming two-step process; instead, teach the dog to sit to a verbal request or hand signal from the outset. Once the dog sits willingly when requested, by all means use your hands to pet the dog when she does so.

To teach down when the dog is already sitting, say "Fido, down!," hold the lure in one hand (palm down) and lower that hand to the floor between the dog's forepaws. As the dog lowers her head to follow the lure, slowly move the lure away from the dog just a fraction (in front of her paws). The dog will lie down as she stretches her nose forward to follow the lure. Praise the dog when she does so. If the dog stands up, you pulled the lure away too far and too quickly.

When teaching the dog to lie down from the standing position, say "Down" and lower the lure to the floor as before. Once the dog has lowered her forequarters and assumed a play bow, gently and slowly move the lure towards the dog between her forelegs. Praise the dog as soon as her rear end plops down.

After just a couple of trials it will be possible to alternate sits and downs and have the dog energetically perform doggy push-ups. Praise the dog a lot, and after half a dozen or so push-ups reward the dog with a training treat or toy. You will notice the more energetically you move your arm—upwards (palm up) to get the dog to sit, and downwards (palm down) to get the dog to lie down—the more energetically the dog responds to your requests. Now try training the dog in silence and you will notice she has also learned to respond to hand signals. Yeah! Not too shabby for the first session.

To teach stand from the sitting position, say "Fido, stand," slowly move the lure half a dog-length away from the dog's nose, keeping it at nose level, and praise the dog as she stands to follow the lure. As soon as the dog stands, lower the lure to just beneath the dog's chin to entice her to look down; otherwise she will stand and then sit immediately. To prompt the dog to stand from the down position, move the lure half a dog-length upwards and away from the dog, holding the lure at standing nose height from the floor.

Teaching rollover is best started from the down position, with the dog lying on one side, or at least with both hind legs stretched out on the same side. Say "Fido, bang!" and move the lure backwards and alongside the dog's muzzle to her elbow (on the side of her outstretched hind legs). Once the dog looks to the side and backwards, very slowly move the lure upwards to the dog's shoulder and backbone. Tickling the dog in the goolies (groin area) often invokes a reflex-raising of the hind leg as an appeasement gesture, which facilitates the tendency to roll over. If you move the lure too quickly and the dog jumps into the standing position, have patience and start again. As soon as the dog rolls onto her back, keep the lure stationary and mesmerize the dog with a relaxing tummy rub.

To teach rollover-stay when the dog is standing or moving, say "Fido, bang!" and give the appropriate hand signal (with index finger pointed and thumb cocked in true Sam Spade fashion), then in one fluid movement lure her to first lie down and then rollover-stay as above.

Teaching the dog to stay in each of the above four positions becomes a piece of cake after first teaching the dog not to worry at the toy or treat training lure. This is best accomplished by hand feeding dinner kibble. Hold a piece of kibble firmly in your hand and softly instruct "Off!" Ignore any licking and slobbering for however long the dog worries at the treat, but say "Take it!" and offer the kibble *the instant* the dog breaks contact with her muzzle. Repeat this a few times, and then up the ante and insist the dog remove her muzzle for one whole second before offering the kibble. Then progressively refine your criteria and have the dog not touch your hand (or treat) for longer and longer periods on each trial, such as for two seconds, four seconds, then six, ten, fifteen, twenty, thirty seconds and so on.

The dog soon learns: (1) worrying at the treat never gets results, whereas (2) noncontact is often rewarded after a variable time lapse.

Teaching "Off!" has many useful applications in its own right. Additionally, instructing the dog not to touch a training lure often produces spontaneous and magical stays. Request the dog to stand-stay, for example, and not to touch the lure. At first set your sights on a short two-second stay before rewarding the dog. (Remember, every long journey begins with a single step.) However, on subsequent trials, gradually and progressively increase the length of stay required to receive a reward. In no time at all your dog will stand calmly for a minute or so.

WALK BY YOUR SIDE

Many people attempt to teach a dog to heel by putting her on a leash and physically correcting the dog when she makes mistakes. There are a number of things seriously wrong with this approach, the first being that most people do not want precision heeling; rather, they simply want the dog to follow or walk by their side. Second, when physically restrained during "training," even though the dog may grudgingly mope by your side when "handcuffed" on leash, let's see what happens when she is off leash. History! The dog is in the next

82

This Aussie is being trained to pick the object with her owner's scent on it from among the others.

county because she never enjoyed walking with you on leash and you have no control over her off leash. So let's just teach the dog off leash from the outset to want to walk with us. Third, if the dog has not been trained to heel, it is a trifle hasty to think about punishing the poor dog for making mistakes and breaking heeling rules she didn't even know existed. This is simply not fair! Surely, if the dog had been adequately taught how to heel, she would seldom make mistakes and hence there would be no need to correct the dog. Remember, each mistake and each correction (punishment) advertise the trainer's inadequacy, not the dog's. The dog is not stubborn, she is not stupid and she is not bad. Even if she were, she would still require training, so let's train her properly.

Let's teach the dog to enjoy following us and to want to walk by our side off leash. Then it will be easier to teach high-precision off-leash heeling patterns if desired. Before going on outdoor walks, it is necessary to teach the dog not to pull. Then it becomes easy to teach on-leash walking and heeling because the dog already wants to walk with you, she is familiar with the desired walking and heeling positions and she knows not to pull.

FOLLOWING

Start by training your dog to follow you. Many puppies will follow if you simply walk away from them and maybe click your fingers or chuckle. Adult dogs may require additional enticement to stimulate them to follow, such as a training lure or, at the very least, a lively trainer. To teach the dog to follow: (1) keep walking and (2) walk away from the dog. If the dog attempts to lead or lag, change pace; slow down if the dog forges too far ahead, but speed up if she lags too far behind. Say "Steady!" or "Easy!" each time before you slow down and "Quickly!" or "Hustle!" each time before you speed up, and the dog will learn to change pace on cue. If the dog lags or leads too far, or if she wanders right or left, simply walk quickly in the opposite direction and maybe even run away from the dog and hide.

Practicing is a lot of fun; you can set up a course in your home, yard or park to do this. Indoors, entice the dog to follow upstairs, into a bedroom, into the bathroom, downstairs, around the living room couch, zigzagging between dining room chairs and into the kitchen for dinner. Outdoors, get the dog to follow

83

around park benches, trees, shrubs and along walkways and lines in the grass. (For safety outdoors, it is advisable to attach a long line on the dog, but never exert corrective tension on the line.)

Remember, following has a lot to do with attitude—your attitude! Most probably your dog will not want to follow Mr. Grumpy Troll with the personality of wilted lettuce. Lighten up—walk with a jaunty step, whistle a happy tune, sing, skip and tell jokes to your dog and she will be right there by your side.

BY YOUR SIDE

It is smart to train the dog to walk close on one side or the other—either side will do, your choice. When walking, jogging or cycling, it is generally bad news to have the dog suddenly cut in front of you. In fact, I train my dogs to walk "By my side" and "Other side"—both very useful instructions. It is possible to position the dog fairly accurately by looking to the appropriate side and clicking your fingers or slapping your thigh on that side. A precise positioning may be attained by holding a training lure, such as a chew toy, tennis ball, or food treat. Stop and stand still several

times throughout the walk, just as you would when window shopping or meeting a friend. Use the lure to make sure the dog slows down and stays close whenever you stop.

When teaching the dog to heel, we generally want her to sit in heel position when we stop. Teach heel position at the standstill and the dog will learn that the default heel position is sitting by your side (left or right—your choice, unless you wish to compete in obedience trials, in which case the dog must heel on the left).

Several times a day, stand up and call your dog to come and sit in heel position—"Fido, heel!" For example, instruct the dog to come to heel each time there are commercials on TV, or each time you turn a page of a novel, and the dog will get it in a single evening.

Practice straight-line heeling and turns separately. With the dog sitting at heel, teach her to turn in place. After each quarter-turn, half-turn or full turn in place, lure the dog to sit at heel. Now it's time for short straight-line heeling sequences, no more than a few steps at a time. Always think of heeling in terms of sit-heel-sit sequences—start and end with the dog in position and do your best to keep her there when moving.

Progressively increase the number of steps in each sequence. When the dog remains close for 20 yards of straight-line heeling, it is time to add a few turns and then sign up for a happy-heeling obedience class to get some advice from the experts.

No Pulling on Leash

You can start teaching your dog not to pull on leash anywhere—in front of the television or outdoors—but regardless of location, you must not take a single step with tension in the leash. For a reason known only to dogs, even just a couple of paces of pulling on leash is intrinsically motivating and diabolically rewarding. Instead, attach the leash to the dog's collar, grasp the other end firmly with both hands held close to your chest, and stand still—do not budge an inch. Have somebody watch you with a stopwatch to time your progress, or else you will never believe this will work and so you will not even try the exercise, and your shoulder and the dog's neck will be traumatized for years to come.

Stand still and wait for the dog to stop pulling, and to sit and/or lie down. All dogs stop pulling and sit eventually. Most take only a couple of minutes; the all-time record is $22\frac{1}{2}$ minutes. Time how long it takes. Gently praise the dog when she stops pulling, and as soon as she sits, enthusiastically praise the dog and take just one step forwards, then immediately stand still. This single step usually demonstrates the ballistic reinforcing nature of pulling on leash; most dogs explode to the end of the leash, so be prepared for the strain. Stand firm and wait for the dog to sit again. Repeat this half a dozen times and you will probably

Train your dog not to dash out of the door ahead of you.

notice a progressive reduction in the force of the dog's one-step explosions and a radical reduction in the time it takes for the dog to sit each time.

As the dog learns "Sit we go" and "Pull we stop," she will begin to walk forward calmly with each single step and automatically sit when you stop. Now try two steps before you stop. Wooooooo! Scary! When the dog has mastered two steps at a time, try for three. After each success, progressively increase the number of steps in the sequence: try four steps and then six, eight, ten and twenty steps before stopping. Congratulations! You are now walking the dog on leash.

Whenever walking with the dog (off leash or on leash), make sure you stop periodically to practice a few position commands and stays before instructing the dog to "Walk on!" (Remember, you want the dog to be compliant everywhere, not just in the kitchen when her dinner is at hand.) For example, stopping every 25 yards

to briefly train the dog amounts to over 200 training interludes within a single 3-mile stroll. And each training session is in a different location. You will not believe the improvement within just the first mile of the first walk.

To put it another way, integrating training into a walk offers 200 separate opportunities to use the continuance of the walk as a reward to reinforce the dog's education. Moreover, some training interludes may comprise continuing education for the dog's walking skills: Alternate short periods of the dog walking calmly by your side with periods when the dog is allowed to sniff and investigate the environment. Now sniffing odors on the grass and meeting other dogs become rewards which reinforce the dog's calm and mannerly demeanor. Good Lord! Whatever next? Many enjoyable walks together of course. Happy trails!

CHAPTER NINE

Resources

BOOKS

About Australian Shepherds

Hartingale, Joseph. *Australian Shepherds.* Neptune, NJ: TFH Publications, 1996.

Palika, Liz. *Australian Shepherd: Champion of Versatility.* New York: Howell Book House, 1995.

About Health Care

American Kennel Club. *American Kennel Club Dog Care and Training.* New York: Howell Book House, 1991.

Carlson, Delbert, DVM, and James Giffen, MD. *Dog Owner's Home Veterinary Handbook.* New York: Howell Book House, 1992.

DeBitetto, James, DVM, and Sarah Hodgson. *You & Your Puppy.* New York: Howell Book House, 1995.

Lane, Marion. *The Humane Society of the United States Complete Guide to Dog Care.* New York: Little, Brown & Co., 1998.

McGinnis, Terri. *The Well Dog Book.* New York: Random House, 1991.

Schwartz, Stephanie, DVM. *First Aid for Dogs: An Owner's Guide to a Happy Healthy Pet.* New York: Howell Book House, 1998.

Volhard, Wendy and Kerry L. Brown. *The Holistic Guide for a Healthy Dog.* New York: Howell Book House, 1995.

About Training

Ammen, Amy. *Training in No Time.* New York: Howell Book House, 1995.

Benjamin, Carol Lea. *Mother Knows Best.* New York: Howell Book House, 1985.

Bohnenkamp, Gwen. *Manners for the Modern Dog.* San Francisco: Perfect Paws, 1990.

Dunbar, Ian, Ph.D., MRCVS. *Dr. Dunbar's Good Little Book.* James & Kenneth Publishers, 2140 Shattuck Ave. #2406, Berkeley, CA 94704. (510) 658-8588. Order from Publisher.

Evans, Job Michael. *People, Pooches and Problems.* New York: Howell Book House, 1991.

Palika, Liz. *All Dogs Need Some Training.* New York: Howell Book House, 1997.

Volhard, Jack and Melissa Bartlett. *What All Good Dogs Should Know: The Sensible Way to Train.* New York: Howell Book House, 1991.

About Activities

Hall, Lynn. *Dog Showing for Beginners.* New York: Howell Book House, 1994.

O'Neil, Jackie. *All About Agility.* New York: Howell Book House, 1998.

Simmons-Moake, Jane. *Agility Training, The Fun Sport for All Dogs.* New York: Howell Book House, 1991.

Vanacore, Connie. *Dog Showing: An Owner's Guide.* New York: Howell Book House, 1990.

Volhard, Jack and Wendy. *The Canine Good Citizen.* New York: Howell Book House, 1994.

MAGAZINES

The AKC GAZETTE, The Official Journal for the Sport of Purebred Dogs
American Kennel Club
260 Madison Ave.
New York, NY 10014
www.akc.org

Dog Fancy
Fancy Publications
3 Burroughs
Irvine, CA 92618
(714) 855-8822
http://dogfancy.com

Dog World
Maclean Hunter Publishing Corp.
500 N. Dearborn, Ste. 1100
Chicago, IL 60610
(312) 396-0600
www.dogworldmag.com

PetLife: Your Companion Animal Magazine
Magnolia Media Group
1400 Two Tandy Center
Fort Worth, TX 76102
(800) 767-9377
www.petlifeweb.com

Dog & Kennel
7-L Dundas Circle
Greensboro, NC 27407
(336) 292-4047
www.dogandkennel.com

MORE INFORMATION ABOUT AUSTRALIAN SHEPHERDS

National Breed Club

UNITED STATES AUSTRALIAN SHEPHERD ASSOCIATION
Corresponding Secretary:
Andrea Blizzard
34 Decktown Tpke.
Sussex, NJ 07461

Breed Rescue:
Second Time Around Aussie Rescue
(STAAR)
Kyle Trumbul-Clark
(805) 270-0702

The association can send you information on all aspects of the breed, including the names and addresses of breed clubs in your area, as well as obedience clubs. Inquire about membership.

The American Kennel Club

The American Kennel Club (AKC), devoted to the advancement of purebred dogs, is the oldest and largest registry organization in this country. Every breed recognized by the AKC has a national (parent) club. National clubs are a great source of information on your breed. The affiliated clubs hold AKC events and use AKC rules to hold performance events, dog shows, educational programs, health clinics and training classes. The AKC staff is divided between offices in New York City and Raleigh, North Carolina. The AKC has an excellent Web site that provides information on the organization and all AKC-recognized breeds. The address is www.akc.org.

For registration and performance events information, or for customer service, contact:

THE AMERICAN KENNEL CLUB
5580 Centerview Dr., Suite 200
Raleigh, NC 27606
(919) 233-9767

The AKC's executive offices and the AKC Library (open to the public) are at this address:

THE AMERICAN KENNEL CLUB
260 Madison Ave.
New York, New York 10014
(212) 696-8200 (general information)
(212) 696-8246 (AKC Library)
www.akc.org

AMERICAN RARE BREED ASSOCIATION
9921 Frank Tippett Rd.
Cheltenham, MD 20623
(301) 868-5718 (voice or fax)
www.arba.org

CANADIAN KENNEL CLUB
89 Skyway Ave., Ste. 100
Etobicoke, Ontario
Canada M9W 6R4
(416) 675-5511
www.ckc.ca

ORTHOPEDIC FOUNDATION FOR ANIMALS (OFA)
2300 E. Nifong Blvd.
Columbia, MO 65201-3856
(314) 442-0418
www.offa.org/

UNITED KENNEL CLUB
100 E. Kilgore Rd
Kalamazoo, MI 49001-5598
(616) 343-9020
www.ukcdogs.com

Trainers

Animal Behavior & Training Associates (ABTA)
9018 Balboa Blvd., Ste. 591
Northridge, CA 91325
(800) 795-3294
www.Good-dawg.com

Association of Pet Dog Trainers (APDT)
(800) PET-DOGS
www.apdt.com

National Association of Dog Obedience Instructors (NADOI)
729 Grapevine Highway, Ste. 369
Hurst, TX 76054-2085
www.kimberly.uidaho.edu/nadoi

Associations

Delta Society
P.O. Box 1080
Renton, WA 98507-1080

(Promotes the human/animal bond through pet-assisted therapy and other programs) www.petsform.com/ DELTASOCIETY/dsi400.htm

Dog Writers Association of America (DWAA)
Sally Cooper, Secretary
222 Woodchuck Lane
Harwinton, CT 06791
www.dwaa.org

National Association for Search and Rescue (NASAR)
4500 Southgate Place, Ste. 100
Chantilly, VA 20157
(703) 222-6277
www.nasar.org

Therapy Dogs International
6 Hilltop Rd.
Mendham, NJ 07945

OTHER USEFUL RESOURCES— WEB SITES

General Information— Links to Additional Sites, On-Line Shopping

www.k9web.com – resources for the dog world

www.netpet.com – pet related products, software and services

www.apapets.com – The American Pet Association

www.dogandcatbooks.com – book catalog

www.dogbooks.com – on-line bookshop

www.animal.discovery.com/ – cable television channel on-line

Health

www.avma.org – American Veterinary Medical Association (AVMA)

www.aplb.org – Association for Pet Loss Bereavement (APLB)—contains an index of national hot lines for on-line and office counseling.

www.netfopets.com/AskTheExperts. html – veterinary questions answered on-line.

Breed Information

www.bestdogs.com/news/ – newsgroup

www.cheta.net/connect/canine/breeds/ – Canine Connections Breed Information Index

Activity, necessity of, 2-3, 5
Allergies, 25-26, 37
American Kennel Club (AKC), 47-48, 51
Appetite, loss of, 24, 28
Ascarids (roundworms), 20-21
Autoimmune disease, 30-31

Bald/hot spots, 29
Barking, 74-77
Bathing, 42-43
Bedding, 8-10
Bee stings, 27
Biscuits/treats, 40, 76
Bleeding, 25, 30
Bloat, 31
Body, 51
Bones, broken, 25-26
Bordatella vaccine, 19
Bowls, 8, 10
Breeding standards, 47-48
    body, 51
    classifications, 59
    color, 52
    ears, 51
    expression, 50
    eyes, 50
    gait, 53
    head, 49-50
    neck, 51
    proportion, 53
    size, 53
    substance, 53-54
    teeth, 50-51
    temperament, 49
Brushing, 42
Burns, 25, 30

Cancer, 31
Canned food, 40
Chewing, 8-9, 70, 75-77
Children, 1-2
Choking, 27-29
Coat
    bathing, 42-43
    brushing, 43

condition, 15-16
shedding, 5-6, 41
Coccidiosis, 20, 22
Collars, 8, 10, 70
Color/markings, 52
Come and sit command, 77-78
Confinement, 8-10, 72-74
Coronavirus, 19
Coughing, kennel, 19, 28
Crates
    bedding, 8-10
    training, 13-14, 72-74
Cuts/scratches, 27

Dehydration, 25-26
Dental hygiene. See Teeth
DHLPP vaccine, 18-20
Diarrhea, 25-26, 28
Down command, 79-81
Dry feeding, 39-40

Ears, 17, 29, 43, 51
Emergencies. See First aid
Energy, loss of, 28
Exercise, 3-5, 16
Expression, 50
Eyes, 17-18, 31, 50

First aid. See also Health care
    bee stings, 27
    bleeding, 25, 30
    broken bones, 25-26
    burns, 25, 30
    choking, 27-29
    contacting veterinarians, 25
    dehydration, 25-26
    diarrhea, 25-26, 28
    energy, loss of, 28
    heatstroke, 25, 27
    poisonous substances, 26
    scratches/cuts, 27
    vomiting, 24-25, 28
Flea control, 18
Following while walking, 83-84

Food
    allergies, 25-26, 37
    amount, 37-38
    appetite, loss of, 24, 28
    bowls, 8, 10
    canned/dry/semimoist, 40
    dry feeding, 39
    establishing routine, 8
    free-feeding, 36
    ingredients, 34-35
    labels, reading, 38
    less active dogs, 35
    life-stage feeding, 34-35
    nutritional requirements, 36-37
    obesity, 39-40
    puppies, 8, 33-34
    vitamin supplements, 39
    wet feeding, 38
Free-feeding, 36

Gait, 53
Genetic ailments, 30-32
Giardia, 20, 22
Grooming. See also Health care
    coat, 6
    nails, 44-46
    schedule, 15
    supplies, 7, 10
Guide dogs, 63

Head
    shaking, 29
    shape, 49-50
Health care. See also First aid; Grooming
    appetite, loss of, 24, 28
    ears, 17, 29, 43
    eyes, 17-18, 31
    flea control, 18
    internal parasites, 20-23
    neutering, 23
    preventive, 15-16
    spaying, 23
    teeth, 29, 44
    tick control, 16-18
    vaccinations, 18-20

Heartworms, 20, 22-23
Heatstroke, 25, 27
Heel command, 82-85
Heimlich maneuver, 29
Herding instincts, 1, 56-57
Hip Dysplasia (HD), 32
History
    American West, 59-60
    Australia, 60
    Basque, 60-61
    herding dogs, 57-59
Hookworms, 20-22
Hot/bald spots, 29
Housetraining, 71-75

Identification
    microchips, 8, 11
    tags, 8, 10-11
    tattoos, 8, 11
Intelligence, 4-5
Itching, 29

Kennel cough, 19, 28
Kong chewing toys, 70, 76

Lameness/limping, 29
Leashes, 8, 10, 70, 85-86
Less active dogs, 35
Life-stage feeding, 34-35
Lumps, 16, 29
Lure-reward training,
    67-70, 78

Markings/color, 52
Microchips, identification, 8, 11

Nails, trimming, 44-46
Neck, 51
Neutering, 23
Nutrition. See Food
Nylon chew toys, 9-10

Obesity, 39-40
Off command, 82
Outdoor confinement, 11, 72

Panosteitis, 32
Parasites, internal, 20-23
Parvovirus, 19
Personality
    with children, 1-2
    intelligence, 4-5
    necessity of activity, 2-3
    socialization, 13, 16, 66, 78
    temperament, 49
Play-training, 64, 74
Poisonous substances, 11, 13, 26
Popularity, 24, 61
Potty training, 72-75
Preventive health care, 15-16
Proportion, 53
Protective instincts, 2
Pulling on leash, 85-86
Puppies
    feeding, 8, 33-34
    proofing your home, 10-11
    schedule, 12-13

Rollover-stay command, 80-82
Roundworms (ascarids), 20-21
Routine, establishing, 12-13
Runny nose, 28

Scratches/cuts, 27
Search and rescue abilities, 62
Semimoist food, 40
Service dogs, 63
Shedding, 5-6, 41
Shock, 25
Sit command, 78-79
Size, 3, 53
Socialization, 13, 16, 66, 78
Spaying, 23
Stand command, 80-81
Stockdogs, 61-62
Strength, 3-4

Tags, identification, 8, 10-11
Tapeworms, 20
Tattoos, identification, 8, 11
Tearing in eyes, 18

Teeth
    bite/condition, 50-51
    brushing, 29, 44
Temperament, 49
Therapy dogs, 63
Thyroid disease, 32
Tick control, 16-17
Time outs, 14
Toys, chewing, 9-10, 70, 76-77
Tracking abilities, 62-63
Training
    barking, 74-77
    chewing, 75-77
    come and sit command,
        77-78
    communication, 66-67
    crates, 13-14
    establishing routine, 12-13
    heel command, 82-85
    housetraining, 71-72
    importance of, 64-66
    lure-reward, 67-70, 78
    obedience, 3, 5
    off command, 82
    play-training, 64, 74
    potty training, 72-75
    sit, down, stand and rollover
        command, 79-82
    trainers, 66, 68
Treats, 40, 76

Vaccinations, 18-20
Veterinarians, emergencies, 25
Vitamin supplements, 39
Vomiting, 24-25, 28

Walking
    after elimination, 74-75
    following, 83-84
    heel command, 82-85
Water, 8, 10
Web sites, 90
Weight, 38
Wet feeding, 38
Whipworms, 20, 22

Australian Shepherd

YOUR ESSENTIAL INFORMATION SHEET

Tear me out!

Put a picture of your dog
in this box

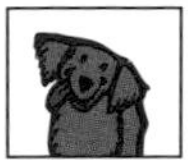

Your Dog's Name

Your Dog's License Number

Date of Birth

Your Dog's Veterinarian

Address

Phone Number

Medications

Vet Emergency Number

Additional Emergency Numbers

Feeding Instructions

Exercise Routine

Favorite Treats

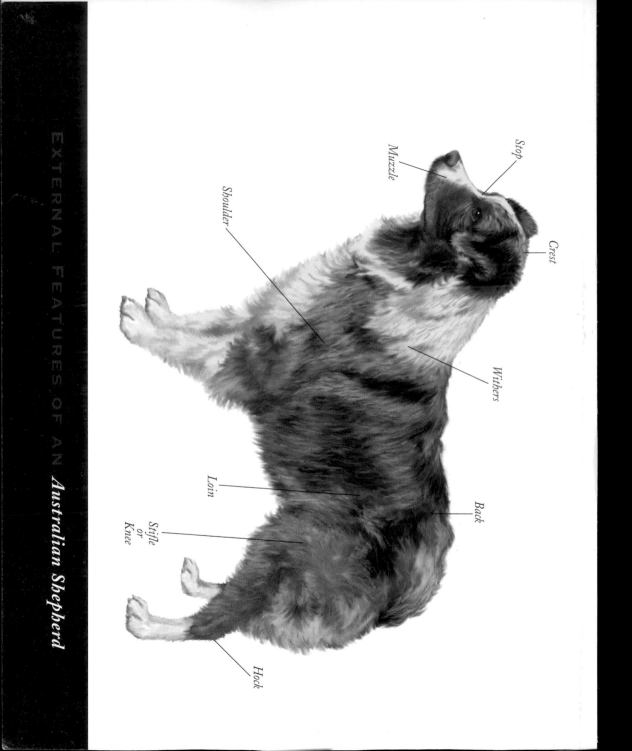

Stop

Muzzle

Crest

Shoulder

Withers

Loin

Back

Stifle
or
Knee

Hock